Living the ABUNDANT *Life*

Living the ABUNDANT Life

By Paula White

Published by
Paula White Ministries

Unless otherwise indicated, all Scripture quotations are taken from the King James Version of the Bible.

Scriptures taken from The Holy Bible, New International Version (NIV), © 1978 by The Zondervan Corporation. Used by permission. All rights reserved.

Scriptures taken from The Holy Bible, The Amplified Bible, © 1983 by The Zondervan Corporation. Used by permission. All rights reserved.

ISBN: 0-9712650-5-4
Copyright © 2003 by Paula White
All rights reserved.

Published by:
Paula White Ministries
P.O. Box 25151
Tampa, FL 33622-5151, USA.

DEDICATION

This book is dedicated to the Lord, my husband, my children and my staff.

To my Lord and Savior, words cannot articulate the magnitude of my love for you for rescuing me from self-destruction and showing me through your love, grace, goodness and mercy how to live the abundant life. Thank you God for this abundant life which is far beyond anything this world has to offer. I am so grateful for this supernatural peace, joy and wholeness in spirit, soul and body for which you sent your son, Jesus, to die.

To my husband, Randy, whom God has used the most to demonstrate His love and grace, words cannot express my love and appreciation for you. You are my soul mate. Thank you for seeing something in me that I could not see. Thank you for believing in me, cultivating me and helping to prepare me for the call of God in my life. You are my best friend, my love, my partner, my mentor, my coach, my high priest and my husband.

To my children, Kristen, Angie, Brandon and Brad, I am so proud of you. You light up my world and bring so much joy to me. As your Dad and I often say, "You are our Rolls Royce." I am fulfilled and satisfied with your love and who you are. You are a reflection of the value of parenting. You make me proud to be your mother.

To my wonderful staff with whom God has blessed me, I could not carry on this ministry without your dedication, hard work and encouragement. God will richly bless you for standing with me to reach this hurting world for Jesus.

TABLE OF CONTENTS

Chapter One—The Principles of Prosperity
Living the Abundant Life *1*
Prosperity Is a God Idea *2*
Reaching the Balance of Success *5*
The Transformation Principle *7*
The Giving Principle *9*
The Measuring Principle *10*
The Kingdom Principle *11*

Chapter Two—Promises of Prosperity
Riches Intended for You *15*
The Promise of Giving and Receiving *17*
The Promise of a Future *19*
The Promise of Wealth *20*

Chapter Three—Keys to Supernatural Finances
Living in the Supernatural *23*
To Prosper or Not? *24*
Motives and Money *26*
The Purpose of Money *29*
Finding Financial Freedom *31*
The Perception of Prosperity *34*

Chapter Four—Keys to Abundant Living
Living through Forgiveness *37*
Knowing the Value of Money *38*
Governed by Your Wealth *40*
Know Who You Are *44*
Using Money Wisely *47*
Wise as Serpents, Gentle as Doves *49*

Chapter 5—The Principles of Covenant
    Delegated Authority *53*
    Covenant of Relationship *54*
    The Good Life *56*
    Covenant 101 .... *58*
    The Abrahamic Covenant *60*

Chapter 6—The Covenant of Tithing
    The Prosperity Perspective *67*
    The Eternal Covenant *71*
    The Tithe Principle *72*
    The Devoted, or First, Things *74*
    The Covenant of the Tithe *78*
    Cursed with a Curse *80*
    Keeping Things in Order,
        the Melchizedek Tithe *86*
    Final Thoughts *90*

Living the ABUNDANT Life

*For I know the thoughts that I think
toward you, saith the Lord, thoughts of peace,
and not of evil, to give you an expected end"
(Jeremiah 29:11).*

Before you were in your mother's womb, you were on the mind of God. He had already destined, chosen, and marked you, because He has a plan for your life. And part of that plan is for you to prosper. What a frustration it is to want to do something for God and be restricted, because you don't have the resources to do what you've dreamed. So you consider in your mind, this thought-provoking possibility. Why not me? Why not now?

God will never give you a vision without giving you the provision. Everything God told you to do, He not only will qualify you to do, but He will also equip you to do. God's people are supposed to live in abundance and overflow! It is not His will for you to just get by from day to day.

As a young girl, my concept of money was distorted. I was conditioned to believe that I did not deserve nice things. When tragedy struck our family, we immediately went from abundant living to poverty. For the first time, my eyes were opened to lack and need. So my earliest memories imbedded into my mind concerning money were negative, based upon our struggles. That opened the door to fear, and it became a mental stronghold to me, an innocent six-year-old girl.

You can't conquer what you don't confront, and you can't confront what you don't identify. I have told my story, how God has blessed Randy and I many times at conferences, Without Walls International Church, and on cassette tape. But what you haven't heard is how God got us where we are today. Our "success" is no secret as we learned to apply some key principles about prosperity along the way.

The Lord has laid it on my heart to shares the promises and principles for Living the Abundant Life. Prosperity is much more than money. In this book you will receive revelation that will change your life forever! So, ask yourself this question: Why not me? Why not now? God declares in John 10:10 His desire for you. Discover the truth about prosperity and learn how to walk in the abundance of God. I trust that the words of this book will inspire you to know that God has an expected end for you life!

Paula White

Chapter One

THE PRINCIPLES
of PROSPERITY

Living the Abundant Life

 *T*o understand the purpose of life and prosperity, we must first understand abundant living. Prosperity is not just money. It is having wholeness and completeness in life. This was the purpose of God when He created man—to give him abundant life. John 10:10 reveals to us the mission statement and purpose of Jesus coming to earth. He came to give you and me life and life more abundantly! The Amplified Version of the Bible says Jesus came so that you would enjoy life to its fullest. And so, the Father's mission's purpose of sending His Son was to give you the abundant life of Christ.

Notice that it doesn't say, "I came to give you heaven." Neither does it say, " I came and died on the cross, then made it so when you got saved, you died and just went to heaven." It is true that there is a place prepared for us, but Jesus' mission was not just for you to make it to heaven. Praise God that we will go to heaven, but there is more to salvation than heaven. In fact, many believers may miss their destiny, because they think that their only purpose in life is to make it to heaven. That's not the case. Your destiny is to fulfill the will of God here on earth, as well as in heaven.

Abundant living for the Israelites was more than Canaan Land. The abundant life was provision in Egypt, in the wilderness, and in the crossing over the Jordan River. God never intended for them to stay in Egypt, but while they were there, He provided a Goshen—a place of protection and provision. He didn't want them to wander in the wilderness, but while they were there, He provided water, quail, and manna. Their ultimate destiny was Canaan, where there were cities they did not build, wells they did not dig, and vineyards they did not plant. (Deut. 6:11.) Egypt was the place of not enough, and the wilderness was the place of just enough, but Canaan was the place of more than enough. It's time you moved into more than enough!

Prosperity Is a God Idea

God's Word is precept upon precept, line upon line principles. The first thing you need to know about walking in supernatural increase is that God wants you to prosper. Now, I know that sounds so simple, but you would be amazed at how many people struggle in their mind with the fact that God wants them to prosper. It's because life teaches you contrary.

Many of us struggle. The struggle is not in preparing the place of prosperity. The struggle is not the place of provision; the struggle is preparing God's people. It always has been. It's like when He was moving the children of Israel out of Egypt. The problem was not to prepare the place. The problem was to prepare the people, nomadic people who were so used to traveling. Some of you have traveled all your life, looking for the blessings of God, but all you've done is survived. You've traveled from this situation, this circumstance, to that; and you're hooked on surviving. But God doesn't just want you to survive.

When the children of Israel got to the Jordan River, the manna stopped. Some of you always want manna. God doesn't want you to live on manna. He doesn't want you to live on miracles. You're not supposed to survive from miracle to miracle to miracle. Miracles, signs, and wonders are for the unbeliever.

God's people are supposed to live in the abundance and the overflow of His goodness, His mercy, and His provision. You're not supposed to have to pray to make it from day to day, day to day, day to day. You're supposed to walk by goodness. What God provided is the supernatural abundant life that Jesus Christ declared when He said, "It is finished."

Psalm 35:27 says, "Yea, let them say continually, Let the Lord be magnified, which hath pleasure in the prosperity of His servant." The context of Psalm 35 is David lamenting to God over those who are mocking him, laughing at him, judging him, and rejoicing in David's flight from his enemies. But despite their gloating, David declares that they will eventually have to admit how good God is to David and will finally declare from their own lips, "Let the Lord be magnified."

Magnify here means, "to swell up or to make large."[1] It's the same Hebrew word used by David when he said, "Oh, magnify the Lord with me and let us exalt his name together," talking about praise. When you begin to praise God, it means He swells up. When your enemies attack you, God will prosper you as you praise Him. When you magnify God, you enlarge your view of Him. Your perspective and view of God becomes bigger than your problem—it swells God up. Despite trouble, He becomes your source.

You have to understand that God is not glorified when you are broke, busted, and disgusted. God is not glorified when you can't put food on your table. God is not glorified when you can't send missionaries out. God is not glorified when you have a dream and no resources to fulfill the dream and the desire in your heart. So the Bible says, "Let the Lord be magnified." Get a picture of this right now. God swells up, because He takes pleasure in the prosperity of His servant. When you prosper, it brings pleasure to God.

Do you want to please God? You wouldn't be reading this if you didn't want to please Him. So, in other words, God says, "I take pleasure when you prosper." That means if you have a problem with prosperity, that's the thing–you have the problem. It's not God. It's you, and it's a mind-set, because poverty is a mind-set. That's the thing we're going to tap deep into, because you can have a lot of "stuff" and still be enslaved in your mind. This is because poverty is not just a condition or state of being; it's a mind-set. God wants you to prosper!

When Randy (my husband) and I moved into Highland Park, I remember the first time, while relaxing in my Jacuzzi tub; I suddenly began to feel guilty. I felt like, "I don't deserve this" ("this" being the luxuries of life). Before I had a chance to become overwhelmed, suddenly the Lord rebuked me and said, "Paula, it has nothing with what you deserve or don't deserve, because it's not because of your works. It is because of the provisions included in the blood covenant that you can sit here today. This has nothing to do with you. It has everything to do with me."

Can you imagine if it was Christmas, and I came to you, and I gave you a gift–and you took that gift and just threw it down? What if you said, "I don't want that. I can't handle that gift." Don't you think I would be offended or hurt? If we don't realize that it was God's idea to bless us in the first place and that every good and every perfect gift cometh down from the Father of lights (James 1:17), then we will not be able to handle His blessings. Because of our mind-sets, because of the way we perceive, because we're enslaved in our minds—we literally reject that which God is trying to bless us with.

Reaching the Balance of Success

God wants us to prosper. In 3 John 2, the beloved John prayed that you would prosper. He said, "Beloved, I wish...." The actual translation for wish means pray, so let's use the word pray [2] ("wish," euchomai). "I pray above all things that thou mayest prosper and be in [good] health, even as thy soul prospereth." This is critical right here as I lay this foundation "I wish above all things that thou would prosper." The Greek word for prosper comes from two words. The prefix is the Greek word eu, which means to be happy, and from the root word odos, a way or path, also a journey.[3] It literally means to find happiness in your journey. It can also mean to succeed in reaching.

God is saying, "Above everything, I want you to succeed when you reach. If you reach for your family, I

5

want to slap success on it. If you'll reach for a dream, I'm going to slap success on it. If you'll reach for ministry, I'm going to slap on success. If you'll reach for business, I'm going to slap on success." In other words, whatever you go for, God is going to cause it to succeed. God takes pleasure in the prosperity of his servants—He wants you to succeed.

So, in 3 John 2 where it says, "Above all things, I wish thou would prosper," it means to succeed in reaching and be in [good] health. And health is not just the physical, it's spiritual.[4] It's a word very similar to Shalom in the Hebrew, which literally means wholeness in your life, prosperity in your life.[5] Prosperity is not just materialism, but it includes materialism in your life. Prosperity carries the idea of wholeness—spirit, soul, mind, safety, and protection.

"I wish thou would prosper as thy soul prospers." It appears that John is trying to say that God desires for every area of your life to prosper. He says, "I wish that you would have a balanced life." John is telling us that we can live in the same degree in our business affairs, in our family affairs, in all of our life affairs, as our soul prospers. So, if your soul is depleted, your business will be depleted, and your family's going to be depleted. This is because your affairs in life should be a reflection of the condition of your soul.

All of your affairs in life are a reflection of the prosperity of your soul. Your soul is your mind, will, and emotions. If your soul doesn't prosper, then your business doesn't prosper, your family doesn't prosper, your ministry doesn't prosper, and your marriage doesn't prosper. Everything becomes a reflection of your soul.

That' why Romans 12:1-2 tells you to present yourself as a "living sacrifice, holy, and acceptable unto the Lord, which is your reasonable service." The Scripture continues, "And be not conformed to this world: but be ye transformed by the renewing of your mind." Renewing is renovation.[6] Renovation is more than learning. It's changing, because renovation is taking away the old and putting in the new. It goes on, "By the renewing [renovation] of your mind, that ye may prove." It is to test, to allow the perfect– complete, good, and acceptable—will of the Lord. My life is a reflection of the prosperity of my soul.

As your soul prospers, so does everything else. Your health prospers, and you succeed in reaching as your soul prospers. So you can say, "I'm the head and not the tail," but you're going to be the tail until your soul prospers. You can say, "I'm going to lend and not borrow." You're going to borrow and pay that crazy interest only for the rest of your life—until you learn how to walk in a prosperous soul.

So if your soul prospers, all areas of your life should be impacted. Something's wrong if you haven't changed in ten years. You should go from glory to glory to glory. You should be different today than you were last week, because the Word should be activated and working on the inside of your life. And that Word operating is manifesting God, because it is bringing completeness to my soul, which brings refreshing in your life.

The Transformation Principle

Everything in your life is a reflection of prosperity, which means you've got to work on your mind. Now,

Philippians 4:8 says, "Whatsoever things are true, whatsoever things are honest, whatsoever things are just, whatsoever things are lovely, whatsoever things are of good report; if there be any virtue, and if there be any praise, think on these things." As your mind is transformed, you will see a reflection of that in your business affairs and health.

You have to constantly think the thoughts of God. Now, does God ever think lack? Show me one Scripture where God thinks lack. Does God ever think decrease? Show me one Scripture where God thinks decrease. Does God ever think poverty? Is God moved by situations and circumstances? Then, you've got to think like God thinks.

The reason I have the marriage I have is because my soul prospers, because as I became whole, my marriage became whole. As I became whole, my finances became whole. As I became whole through the Word of God, my ministry became whole.

Psalm 115:12 says, The Lord hath been mindful of us: he will bless us; he will bless the house of Israel; he will bless the house of Aaron." I need to declare, "The Lord remembers me, and he will bless the house of Paula White. Psalm 115: 14 continues, The Lord shall increase you more and more, you and your children." I need to proclaim, The Lord will increase me and my children more and more." I have to start thinking like God thinks.

So, what's prosperity of the soul? The Greek word for soul in 3 John 2 is psyche.[7] So, you must learn to use your faith correctly to develop life to its fullness. Your soul prospers as you allow the grafted Word of God to change you. The Word of God is the catalyst to your change. This is how we're going to get in the Word for

8

your finances. If your soul is being transformed, then you ought to demand equity in the other areas of your life. All areas should be equitable.

The Giving Principle

God promises to prosper you when you give. It is a season of reaping. Now, I'm focusing on finances, but it's much more than finances. It's everything. The whole kingdom, the system of God, operates by sowing and reaping. When God wanted a family, He sowed a Son, Jesus Christ. The Bible says if you want a friend, you have to be friendly.

God gave man two gifts in the book of Genesis. He gave them dominion, and He gave them authority. (Genesis 1:26.) What can a man do with dominion and authority? You go, "I know, but Satan took it." I know, but Jesus came and got it back for us. So, He gave us dominion, and He gave us authority. I have dominion, and I have authority, and I have seed.

He gave them seed, every herb bearing seed. You have been given dominion, authority and seed—so then you can plant your seed in life—not just financially, but in every area. Then I can determine my own outcome in life, because everything is based on sowing and reaping. Galatians 6:7 tells us, "Be not deceived; God is not mocked, for whatsoever a man soweth, that shall he also reap." So God promises to prosper you when you give, because God's system is different than man's system.

Again, you've got to work on your mind-set, because you've been taught, through life, to take, take, and take. But you've got to retrain your thinking to give, give, and give! Luke 6:48 emphasizes giving for living. If you don't give, then you can't quote the rest of the Scripture. "Give, and it shall be given back to you; good measure, pressed down and shaken together and running over, shall men give into your bosom." To understand the Eastern term "bosom," we must first understand their attire. They wore a long flowing garment, bound by the waist by a girdle, which provided a convenient carrying place for their money bag.[8] This word often refers to this pocket where bread, grain, and even lambs were carried (Ex. 4:6,7; Prov. 17:23; Isa. 40:11).

So, in other words, it says, "When I give from my money bag or, literally, pocket, it shall be given back to the place where I contain and carry my money." Give, and it shall be given back to me, pressed down, shaken together and running over, in good measure shall men give unto Paula White.

When you quote this verse next time, place your name where I placed mine. Make it personal. I learned a long time ago that the Scriptures are for me. You've got to put your name on these Scriptures. I put my name on every one of these Scriptures. And so, if I don't give, then it can't come back to me, running over, pressed down, and shaken together.

The Measuring Principle

The Bible tells us that God enables us to perform the gifts according to the proportion, or measure of faith. The measuring cup of our success is according to that which God has deposited into us. This spiritual principle is true and can be applied to us when it comes to operating within the principles of reaping. Our level of operation is according to what we deposit into God's system.

Matthew 7:2 says, "With what measure ye mete, it shall be measured to you again." So, in other words, if you give an ounce, an ounce or more comes back. If you give a cup, a cup or more comes back. If you give a gallon, a gallon comes back. So, people want a gallon but have an ounce mentality of giving. So, don't get jealous of someone receiving a gallon when you're over here giving an ounce. YOU are determining what's coming back to you. God says in Acts 10:34 that He "is no respecter of persons." God has no more respect for one person than He does for another. We're all equal in His eyes. God does not show favoritism but He does show favor to those who give accordingly.

It's imperative that the body of Christ learn to share the gifts and the blessings of God with each other and not be critical. If you get jealous of others, it will cripple your spirit, and that means that you're depleted. And if you're depleted in your soul, you're depleted in life! It all balances here. So if somebody gets a gallon, it's because they're giving a gallon according to that measure.

The Kingdom Principle

Malachi 3:10 states, "Bring ye all the tithes into the storehouse, that there may be meat in mine house." So God says, "Not only am I going to prosper you, but I'm going to allow the kingdom to go forth as you invest into it. God wants you to prosper. He gives you His prosperous kingdom.

The kingdom of God is not just referring to heaven.[9] The kingdom is royalty and the realm of God. John the Baptist preached, "Repent, for the kingdom of heaven is at hand." (Matt. 3:2.) Jesus declared the same as John. (Matt. 4:17.) In other words, God's way of doing things, His system, is now in operation. You don't wait until you die to live by the principles that operate in the kingdom of God.

You don't have to die to operate in kingdom principles. You can walk in them right now. That's why I'm not bound by natural laws. That's why I can say things and watch them come to pass. That's why if I have faith as a grain of mustard seed that I can move a mountain. (Lk. 17:6.)

A seed planted never leaves you. It just goes into your future. So, you can't be so mindful of today's situation and circumstances that you don't focus on what is ahead of you. Live for today, but dream for tomorrow. A seed planted leaves you and goes into your future.

The natural realm does not bind you. That's why you can speak to a storm and the storm has to cease. (Mark 4:37-39.) That's why greater works than Jesus will you do. (John 14:12.) That's why the same anointing that was on Jesus is now upon you, because you have been called and commissioned to walk in that anointing, and that increase, and that supernatural abundance. You're not bound by natural laws. You live by kingdom principles that supersede any natural principles, because Jesus said, "I come to give you life and life more abundantly." (Jn. 10:10.)

To repent is to change your way of doing things. To repent is not just you saying, "I'm sorry." To repent means to do a 180-degree turn.[10] Prior, you were doing it this way, but now you begin to do it this way–and watch how God's promises come to pass in your life. Luke 12:32 says, "It is your Father's good pleasure to give you the kingdom."

I believe there are some people who are going to get to heaven, and there are going to be gifts all laid up. And they'll say, "Well, what are all those gifts doing over there?" And it will be said, "The Father had them assigned to you for your possession, and He tried to release them to you, but you never asked for them." I believe God has some stuff on lay away, and He is waiting for you to come and claim them. You won't need those gifts in heaven; you need those gifts here on earth. When you get to heaven, what are you going to need them for? To whom are you going to be prophesying? You'll have your mansion. You'll have sidewalks and streets of gold. What are you going to be using faith for in heaven? Your faith is to be used down here. He has given you a measure of faith.

God has also given you gifts. He's given you gifts that you're supposed to activate and operate in. Nobody said it would come easy. In fact, in Mark 10:28, Peter said, "We have left all." And Jesus answered, "There is nothing you have left, not houses, not brothers, not sister, that you will not have a hundredfold return and eternal life in this life, with persecution." That's the problem. God said, "You're going to get it, but it's going to come with persecution." The enemy doesn't want you to walk in it. That's okay. Who cares about the giants in the land? Just go forth in grace. Go for your stuff. Go for your anointing. Go for your family. Go for your increase. Go for your supernatural abundance.

Chapter Two

PROMISES
of PROSPERITY

Riches Intended for You

*G*od gives you good things that the wicked want. God wants to add these things to you, the things that the wicked seek out. He's not trying to withhold anything from you, He wants to bless you. What kind of father would He be if He wanted to withhold things, if he just wanted you to be spiritual? If God just wanted you to be spiritual, all you would be is a spirit.

Don't let the devil mess with your head. "Well, he lied on me." He's supposed to. He is the father of lies. (Jn. 8:44.) Beware when all men speak well of you. He's supposed to lie on you. "Well, this person talked about me, and then this person talked about me. And you should've seen the look she gave me when I drove up in my new car." They're supposed to. It is supposed to come with persecution.

God desires to give you material things. Matthew 6:33 says, "Seek ye first the kingdom of God and his righteousness." The Scripture continues, "and all these things shall be added unto you." Now, what does "all these things" refer to? It is referring to a prior verse,

15

verse 31. It says, in effect, "Don't worry about what you're going to eat, where you're going to sleep, what you're going to wear," yet we would agree that those things are pretty important to maintain a normal day in life.

Then, when it pertains to what you're going to eat, God said, "Don't worry about those things, for the heathen (that don't even know me), they seek after these things." Your heavenly Father knows that you have need of such things. He'll take care of you. Verse 26 says, "Behold the fowls of the air: for they sow not neither do they reap, nor gather into barns; yet your heavenly Father feedeth them. Are you not much better than they?" In other words, they're not privileged to God's system of sowing and reaping, and yet, He provides for them. But you're privileged to the kingdom's principles, so how much more will God add things in your life when you begin to operate by kingdom principles? When you know how to sow, you understand how also to reap in life.

God wants you to have good things. He gives you everything you need, the best of spiritual and natural things. second Peter 1:3 tells us that "His divine power hath given unto us all things that pertain unto life [natural] and godliness [spiritual]." So God will give you an anointing for natural things, and God will give you an anointing for spiritual things. He wants you blessed in every area of your life.

You can run a multimillion-dollar company. You can go in like Daniel in the lion's den, right in the midst of those lions. They won't even touch you, because you have so much wisdom in your mouth. They won't even know what to do with you. You'll be like Jesus. You can escape their threats, and you'll be just like when they tried to push Him over a cliff. There'll be a corporate take over, and you'll just walk out from the midst of them, because you're so anointed for business. You can be spiritual and be smart. You can be spiritual and know how to take a dollar and turn it into a thousand.

When I was young, in fourth grade, my brother and I wanted to start our own businesses. We discovered that if we opened up a little casino in our bedroom, we could make more money. So, we put beads up and a craps table. We charged 75 cents to come in, as a cover charge. Now, if I had enough business sense to make money at age 10 through worldly means, what can God do through me for the kingdom?

As a spirit-filled Christian who knows how to make money, by legal and moral means, what can happen now that I can do something good for God? I knew how to market a lemonade stand as a child. I knew how to stand there and get everybody's quarter. But I can see how God was training me for my destiny. You can be spiritual and still make money. Some Christians do not know that you can be spiritual and still drive a nice car.

The Promise of Giving and Receiving

God is a giver, and He sets the example, which we should follow. The Amplified Bible says, "Therefore be imitators of God–copy Him and follow His example–as well-beloved children [imitate their father]." (Eph. 5:1.) It is obvious that we should imitate God. Our lives should be reflections of Him. We should think like God, talk like God, walk like God, and give like God.

Everything that you feel is your destiny, your desire, your dream, I believe that the Lord will equip you for in life. Imitate, copy Him, and follow Him. Now, this is important, many of us, sometimes we can give, but we have a hard time receiving.

One time somebody spoke into my life at a pivotal time. They gave me a real nice gift, and I was like, "Oh, no, you can't do that." And they said, "You've got pride." I said, "What do you mean, 'I've got pride?' How dare you say I've got pride? I'm so humble, I won't even accept your gift." (I had a hard time receiving.) I could give and give but I couldn't receive. See, humility sometimes can be false pride. He went on and said, "The reason that you have pride, and the reason you have a hard time receiving is because when you give, you are in control. When you receive, you're out of control." He gently imparted this into my spirit when he said, "You don't see yourself the way God sees you, so you think you're imitating God."

God is not just a God that gives; He is also a God who receives. God receives our worship. The Bible says that He seeks for worshippers who will worship Him in spirit and in truth. (Jn. 4:24.) He seeks people who will whisper in His ear with a heart of love, "I love you." God doesn't just want to give to you. He wants to receive from you. It's a reciprocal thing. He says, "I want to bless you, I want to be good to you, but I want you to worship me. I want you to tell me you love me. I want you to spend time with me." It's not just our giving God is interested in; it's our ability to receive, too.

Some people, all they are just takers. They take all the time. They just take everything because of their "welfare mentality." They think life owes them something. Nobody owes you in life. Get rid of the victim mentality before it kills you. A victim mentality means, "I can't succeed until you let me succeed. And I can't get out of this box until you let me get out of this box."

The Promise of a Future

My destiny is way too precious to put it in the hands of somebody else and allow them to control my future. God said in Joshua 1:8 if I speak the Word, meditate on the Word, and do the Word, then I make my way prosperous, and I make my way successful. He already told me in Isaiah 55:9 that, "My ways [are] higher than your ways, and my thoughts [are higher] than your thoughts".

He also has an expected end. (Jer. 29:11.) It means He has a better outcome, a better hope, and a better conclusion for me than I have for myself. If I had written the script, I would have messed it up. God had something better for me than I had for myself. In other words, the life that God has for me is better than the life I could have planned for myself. That's why Ephesians 3:20 says, "Now unto Him that is able to do exceedingly abundantly above all we ask or think, according to the power that worketh in us."

The more the Word is activated, the more I can see things clearly, the more I can perceive things properly, the more I can ask things correctly. If the Word is activated in my life, my soul prospers, and the power of God works in me. I have the right perception. I can ask properly, and I can walk in the will and the way of God, because His course of life is higher, it's better, than I would have chosen for myself. You know you had a dream for yourself, but God's dream is better than your dream. His plan is better than your plan.

The Promise of Wealth

God gives your hands power to get wealth. Deuteronomy 8:18 declares, "Thou shalt remember the Lord thy God." To remember has to do with you fulfilling your vows and covenants. It means bring to God what belongs to God. The Scripture continues, "For it is he that giveth thee power to get wealth." God gives you an anointing to get wealth.

God wants to give you wealth. But wealth is different than riches. When God says you are going to be wealthy, what does that encompass? When God said, "I'm going to give you power to get wealth"—I believe that He has an anointing for it. But the purpose of wealth is, "that he may establish his covenant which he sware unto thy fathers, as it is this day." God says, "I'm doing this to perform my word and to establish my covenant." It's for His purposes and His plan.

God gives you ways to prosper. Proverb 8:12 says, "I wisdom dwell with prudence, and find out knowledge of witty inventions." God can teach you how to make a profit. Isaiah 48:17 states, "I am the Lord thy God which teacheth thee to profit, which leadeth thee by the way that thou shouldest go." God is saying, "I'll teach you to profit, and I'll lead you the way you should go." In other words, He is going to lead you through the door. Revelations 1:8 says He opens doors that no man can shut. And I truly believe God can put you at the right place at the right time to meet the right person. I believe that He is ordering, confirming, and directing your footsteps.

I truly believe that as you yield yourself, obey the Word of God, and live a lifestyle of giving that you will find your purpose. Your purpose and God's destiny intertwine, leading you to His perfect will. There is nothing more satisfying than knowing you are in the perfect plan of your life. When you discover that God gives you the power to get wealth, you will have arrived at a desire to establish His covenant.

You can't give one time or you won't get a harvest. It's a lifestyle of continual giving. Your whole life is about giving, and not just financially. You're giving kind words, you're giving of your time, and you're giving of things that would equate to money.

My time is as valuable as my money; my time equates to money. I've got to give finances too, but it's a lifestyle of giving. It's giving the wisdom that God gave me. I have wisdom because Bishop Jakes has spoken wisdom into my life. Dr. Lowry has spoken into my life. Miles Monroe spoke into my life. Randy White spoke into my life. Suzanne and Benny Hinn spoke into my life. Now, I give the wisdom I have received to people that God has put in my life. Those who have deposited something in me have given me something that is much more valuable than rubies, diamonds, gold, and silver. The wisdom that they've spoken into my life will lead me the right way. It will keep me from going to the left when I should go to the right. Because I have received their deposit, my lifestyle is all about giving.

At all times you should have a mentor speaking wisdom into your life. Your mentor wants you to learn for their lessons. What you've learned in life is much more valuable than what you've earned in life. If I give you a check, you are limited. If I give you what enabled me to profit instead, and I give you the wisdom that brought me to the place where I am today, then I'm giving you something greater. If I just give you something, I've limited you in life. If I just write you a check, I've limited you. If I give you how I've gotten to live in abundance and overflow and all the wisdom that's been deposited into my life, then I've given you something significant.

You can distinguish whether people are true protégées or not by seeing if they want what you've learned and not what you've earned. They will start coming around you saying things like, "You deserved it," and, "When's my blessing going to come through?" or, "When's my breakthrough?" They are not protégées. All they want is what you've earned not what you've learned. They don't want to take the principles and work the principles to bring the promises.

If you teach me the principles, I can work the principles, and then I won't just have your promise. I'll have my promise. Maybe my promise is bigger than what I see you walking in, so I'm not going to limit myself in life. Teach me the principles, and I can see the promises come to pass. By applying the principles of wisdom, you discover the keys of reaping and sowing and how to get wealth.

Chapter Three

KEYS *to*
SUPERNATURAL
FINANCES

Living in the Supernatural

*G*od wants you to live a supernatural life. "How do I do that, Paula," you may ask? Ephesians 3:20 says, "Now unto Him that is able to do exceedingly abundantly above all we ask or think, according to the power that [is activated] or worketh in us" (emphasis mine). The powerful principles in this chapter concerning your finances will help you in practical ways as you discover life in the supernatural.

You may have a thousand dollar vision. This means your vision will take a thousand dollars of resources, and if you fulfill that vision, you will be successful in life. Or, you may have a multimillion-dollar vision, and it's going to take millions of dollars to fulfill the vision that God has mandated upon your life. If you fulfill that vision, then you will be successful in life.

Money is just a vehicle. It is just a tool. Money is just a way, a means, through which God allows you to accomplish what you need to accomplish according to His purpose and your destiny. I believe you define success as having enough resources to do what God has called you to do in life. It's not the amount; it's the fact that you fulfill the assignment of God, which requires enough finances to do what you've been specifically called to do.

Many people think that all you need to do to get wealth is get a better job. In this chapter you will discover that there are principles of the supernatural that can help you find your purpose of prosperity. Many people in the world's system have wealth, but that is not prosperity. Prosperity is more than that. It includes living a full, complete, and happy life.

To Prosper or Not?

It is God's desire that you prosper. Do you remember the emphasis of Psalm 35:27 when it says, "Let the Lord be magnified"? That literally means to swell up. We must magnify the Lord, who has pleasure in the prosperity of His servants. And may I remind you that prosperity is not just a financial word! It is taken from the Hebrew word shalom, which means wholeness.[1] I define it as nothing missing and nothing broken in your life. It is referring to your welfare, your safety, your protection, your prosperity, your provision, your mental state, your emotional state, your physical state, and your spiritual state. David declared that God takes pleasure in you prospering. God is not magnified when you are broke, busted, or disgusted.

Then in John, Chapter 15, it declares that God's disciples will be known by the fruit produced in their lives. That is your spiritual destiny, that you should be fruitful. Then we found out that the apostle John prayed in 3 John 2, "Beloved, I wish"–which is better translated, "I pray."[2]

"I pray above all things that thou mayest prosper." I define this to mean, "to find happiness in your journey and to succeed in reaching." He is saying that we should pray in order to succeed when we reach for something, that we should prosper, and be in good health.

This is a critical point, so I want to briefly re-emphasize some of the necessary thoughts and truths before we go any further. You are to prosper in your soul. (It has been said that your soul is your mind, your will, and your emotions.) When your soul prospers, then your mind is being transformed. You should see a reflection of prosperity transforming all the affairs of your life. Your marriage should prosper. Your business should prosper. Your ministry should prosper. In other words, your whole life should reflect the prosperity of your soul. If your soul is depleted, your life is going to be depleted.

Put a demand on the prosperity of your soul. You can tap into the prosperity because God has made deposits in you. Put a demand on it in all your areas of life. This is absolutely imperative, because as your soul prospers, you start a process of exchange—the exchange—your weakness for His strength. This exchange will allow the grafted Word of God to be deposited within you.

Being prosperous includes everything you do, think, and believe. It means you should be making progress in reaching toward the prize of your high calling in Christ Jesus. So, it's important that you understand God's mind-set for you—prosperity. It is vital to comprehend your success in life begins when you know that He wants you to prosper! I had to drill that into my mind, because you would be shocked at how I used to think and the way I used to perceive God before I studied the Word.

Your mindset and perception of God will determine how you live and what you expect God to do for you. Some people who do not have a proper view of God actually think He is after them. I heard a Pastor say one time that if you had wealth that meant you did not trust God. What kind of statement is that? It takes more faith to allow God to work a work in your life. What a poor excuse to stay in poverty.

You're supposed to take this Word and make this Word work for you. James, Chapter 1:22 says, "Be ye doers of the word, and not hearers only, deceiving your own selves." Be a doer, an imitator, of the Word. So, everything I see the Word saying should be activated in my life.

Motives and Money

One of the first things you've got to do is define what you want from your money. Let me ask you this, "What is the purpose of believing God for finances?" Simply put, money without a purpose is nothing more than materialism. So, you must first define the role of money for your life. You have to understand what you want your money to do for you. You would be shocked at the different answers I have heard over the years. But by asking yourself that question and writing down the answer, you will reveal the motive for money in your life. That's important, because you can't conquer what you don't identify.

It's important for you to find the purpose of money in your life. Motives are absolutely necessary, because if you're not careful, you'll deceive yourself. You may think you are generous, and yet struggle with covetousness. God's purpose is for you to have money so that it can be channeled through you, and not just so you will be blessed. His ultimate purpose is to make you a BLESSING.

It is important that you recognize this, that your motives can determine and dictate your blessing. Once you realize that motives determine why you do what you do, then you can do the right thing. But if you do the right thing for the wrong reason, it will be ineffective and, ultimately, can be destructive in your life. In Matthew 20:20, we have an example of motives in the story of the mother of the sons of Zebedee. "Then came to him the mother of Zebedee's children with her sons"–watch what she does–"worshipping him." That's a great thing to do! She came to Jesus, and she started out right, that is to worship the King of kings and the Lord of lords.

I have heard it said before that worship means to denote "worth-ship." She begins to note that He is worthy. Literally, the Greek word used here for worship is proskuneo, a compound word. It comes from pros, towards, and kuneo, to kiss. It is an act of homage, reverence, and is usually translated "worship."[3] She came to Jesus honoring Him with high regard, not just as a Rabbi, but also as the Messiah. Her approach to Him was with the appearance of humility and obeisance.

Every Sunday, people go to church and, like this woman, say, "I recognize that you are the King of kings and the Lord of lords. I recognize that you are the Son of God. I recognize that you are Jesus, Emmanuel, given to us, God incarnate. I understand that you are the Word in flesh. I recognize the deity, that you are God walking in a humanity. I recognize that, and I worship you." I am sure you would agree that worship is a worthy thing.

She came and started to worship Him, which was the right thing, but watch what the Scriptures reveal. She worshipped Him because she desired a certain thing. We see the action but then we can see the motive by what she asked for. You can do a right thing, but if you have a wrong motive, it will ultimately bring destruction in your own life.

Everything you do has a motive, everything. You worship God for a reason. You give for a reason. You reach out, and you touch other people for a reason. Everything in life has a motive. You got married for a reason. You want a job for a reason. Motives are very important. The Bible goes on to say that she worshiped Him, desiring a certain thing.

And Jesus said, in verse 21, "What wilt that (I do)?" Then, she revealed her true motive. "And she saith unto him, Grant that these my two sons may sit, the one on thy right hand, and the other on the left, in thy kingdom." She had a strong sense that God was in Jesus and that He was about to prepare for the end. But what she thought was going to happen was not going to take place, and would not become a reality. She thought that Jesus would come and would set up His earthly kingdom at that time, but God doesn't work within our system. He doesn't work within our finite minds. God doesn't work within our limitations. He's God and we're not.

He had a different purpose when He was said, "Thy kingdom come." He was saying, "The way God does things is coming to earth. You can operate in a heavenly system while you're living down here in an earthly, natural boundary." God said, "You're not limited because of

My kingdom. My way of doing things has come."

But she's thinking that Jesus Christ will rise up and take over the Roman Empire. The reason she came to Him and started to worship Him is because she wanted her sons to have position.

It's critical that you understand and define your motives, because some things cannot be rewarded to you when your motives are impure. My Bible tells me that wood, hay, and stubble will be burned up, and only that which is pure, only that which has been purged, will actually stand forth. (1 Cor. 3:12,13.) It's critical that you identify your motive with money and deal with your heart.

The Purpose of Money

This next critical questions to ask yourself are, "What is the purpose for money in my life, and can I identify my motives for money?" If you're trying to do a right thing for a wrong reason, God is not going to bless you and allow you to be covetous, greedy, and have a wrong motive. Ultimately, it would destroy you.

The Bible says a man is not defiled from what is on the outward. Jesus said, "It's not what goes in the belly of a man. It's not the outward that defiles him, but it is that which cometh from the heart. It's that which cometh from the inside that defiles him." (Mark 7:15.) The Greek word for defile in this passage is the word koino-o from the noun, koinos, to defile. In the ceremonial sense, it means to render unholy, unclean, to defile.[4] It has been translated pollute, with the idea to corrupt, and to destroy, to defile the man.

You must first identify the purpose of money in your life. It's not wrong for you to want nice things. It's not evil to want a home. It's not a sin to want a nice car. It's not impure to want to send your children to college. But, you need to understand, if your money is just to give you power, if your money is just to be self-satisfying, if your money is just all about you, then you have an impure motive, and God will not bless that. If He did, He would violate His word, and the end result would ultimately be destruction.

The Bible says in 1 Timothy 6:10, "The love of money is the root of all evil." Money is not evil, as some preachers would try to convey. It is the love of money that is the root of all evil. Now, it's critical that you get that, because if you try to "live up to the Jones," you will live on a perpetual "money merry-go-round." Don't try to be something you weren't created to be. Don't fall into the trap of getting yourself in debt while trying to achieve prosperity. You have an assignment; you have a part to play. The critical thing is you play the part!

If God calls you to raise two children and send them to college, and that is your life's assignment, then you need enough resources to send two children to college. But if God has called you to go on television and preach to two-thirds of the world, then you need enough resources to get airtime to go to two-thirds of the world and preach the Gospel.

Now, if I try to fulfill your assignment, or you try to fulfill my assignment, then we have missed God and messed up. The important thing is that you know what God has assigned in your life, you fit jointly together in the body of Christ, and you do what He has called you to do.

Finding Financial Freedom

Your past holds the key to your financial future. Ecclesiastes 1:9 says, "The thing that hath been, it is that which shall be; and that which is done is that which shall be done: and there is no new thing under the sun." The road to financial freedom in your life is not a financial planner. It is not a bigger paycheck. It is not a bank. The road to financial freedom in your life is not found in a paycheck. It's not found in a better job. It's not found in an education. It's not found in investments. It's not found in supernatural doors opening. I know this is going to blow you away, but the road to your financial future is in your head. It's the way you think. It's the way you perceive.

The road to your financial freedom is not in money itself. It's in your perception of money. The road to your financial freedom is not in your job and not in your paycheck. It's not in any of that. It's in your mind. That's why as a man thinketh so shall he become. (Prov. 23:7.) The way you think about money is what it will become to you. The way you perceive it is what it will be to you. That's why you have to understand that God wants you to prosper. So, the way that you latch onto what God desires for you is you become prosperous in your soul, and you put a demand for equity in your life. You demand that everything should match, should be equivalent, to the prosperity of your soul.

You have to identify how you really feel about money. How can you attach feelings to money? It's all about how you feel about money, because you will treat money the way you feel about it. If you go back to your childhood and your earliest memories, you will discover how you developed your perception of money.

Allow me to give you a personal example. When my father committed suicide, our family immediately went from wealthy living to poverty. For the first time, my eyes were opened to lack and need. We had to struggle for everything, from paying the monthly bills to putting food on the table. My mom made very merger wages that year. At an early age and for the first time in my life, I saw poverty. So my earliest memories embedded in my mind concerning money were negative, based upon our struggles. That opened the door to fear, and it became a mental stronghold to me, an innocent five-year-old girl.

Even though now I have discovered that God desires to bless me and I have money, I had to work at it. I was very tight with money. My husband, Randy, would say, "Why are you so tight with money?" The reason I was so tight with money was because when I was five years old, my daddy committed suicide, and fear entered my life that we weren't going to survive. And so, even though God had blessed me, there was no freedom. The problem was never a money issue in my life. The problem was fear in my life.

What emotion comes to you when I say, "money"? Are you excited? Are you angry? Are you shameful? Do you feel worthy? Do you feel unworthy? Do you feel jealous over somebody else's blessing? Do you feel covetousness? Do you feel fearful of your future? Those things are critical for you to identify, because that which has been is that which will be. The root problem is never money in your life. There are deeper issues that hold you back from walking in the fullness of what God wants for you. You have to learn how to get God's concept and get

His mind, so that you will know how to handle your finances.

Maybe you had siblings in your family that every time you went to the Christmas tree, they got a present that was twice the amount of what you got, or carried a better value of security, and it put an unconscious concept in you that you are not worthy—you are not deserving. That translated that you are unworthy to receive, so you have a problem when God gets ready to bless you.

You can't conquer what you don't confront, and you can't confront what you don't identify. You may not even know why you feel the shame you feel or why you feel the guilt you feel. You've got to go way back, because that which has been is that which will be. You've got to identify where the enemy wanted to mess your perception up. Maybe he sent an assignment when you were a child to keep you messed up when you were an adult.

I know one young man that when he was young, about thirteen years old, he went on a church outing with his Sunday school. He admired the Pastor. And there were about twelve young men, and they all went to this little restaurant. They got malts, and fries, and the whole bit. When the bill came, all the eleven kids, with the exception of him, put down five dollars to pay the bill. He didn't he know he was supposed to pitch in and pay the bill, and so he didn't put five dollars down to help pay that bill. Then he felt rejected, because one of the kids said, "What is wrong with you?" He was embarrassed, and it scarred his thinking for years.

To this day, he is an overspender. He will pick up the tab all the time, even if he cannot afford it. He will buy people stuff to prove himself accepted. And he does so much, always buying, that he's got himself in so much debt. And the problem is not money, because he's got a good paying job. The problem in his life is not money. The problem is he's got a problem with rejection. He was embarrassed in front of his peers. He wanted to be accepted, but he didn't have five dollars to contribute. And so, today, when he's thirty-five years old, he's still overcompensating, trying to show he's worthy.

You've got to understand that the issues in your life are not really money issues. You've got to go deeper than just the dollar bill. How do you feel about money? How does money treat you? What was consciously and unconsciously told to you that is your concept, your feeling about money?

The Perception of Prosperity

If you don't respect money, money won't respect you. You have to value money. I'm trying to help somebody get set free. Whom the Son sets free is free indeed. I want to make you think, because the problem is not a lack of money in your life. The problem is perception. If I can change your mind, I can change your way of life. If I can change the way you see things, I can change what you can receive in life.

God took Abraham from a pagan lifestyle and converted his thinking by increasing his view of things. God convinced him to believe for a future home, based upon his perception when He said to Abraham, "Lift up now thine eyes and look all around you," (Gen. 15:5). God was saying to him, "As far as you can see, you can receive it, because if you can't see it, you can't receive it." If I can open your eyes to understanding, then you'll have revelation and enlightenment.

But how do you get beyond the fear of it never coming to pass? You do it the same way you got beyond every other issue in your life. How do you get over feeling unworthy? How do you get over fear of not reaching your potential in God and prosperity to fulfill your vision? You must define your calling, our role in life. You must see the purpose of money.

The question is not why God wants you to prosper. It is rather, "What does God want to fulfill through you because of your prosperity?" Emotions and past experiences with money will often determine the ways we value money in our lives. Do you have any issues to resolve before God can bless you? In the next chapter, you will discover the keys to abundant living.

Chapter Four

KEYS *to*
ABUNDANT LIVING

Living Through Forgiveness

*B*efore you were ever in your mother's womb, God had already destined you, chosen you, and marked you, because He has a plan for your life. And part of that plan and part of that promise is for you to prosper. What a frustration it is to want to do something for God and be restricted, because you don't have the finances or the resources to do what you dream in life.

God never will give you a vision without giving you the provision. Everything God told you to do, He not only will qualify you to do, but He will also equip you to do. He will place it in your hands or place it within your ability. He doesn't just tell you to go forth, He empowers you to walk in it. His resources are for you.

The devil will try to lie to you convincing you, however, that you cannot make it. Satan will attempt to use your past, hurt, your failures, and your flesh as weapons to disqualify you as a candidate for abundant living. Over the last number of years in ministry, I have found one main tool that Satan successfully uses to prevent people from prosperity and abundant living—unforgiveness. The most common thread in blocking the believer from total victory is the inability to forgive.

You may say, "Paula, I can't forgive them. I can't get over the wrong committed against me. I can't get over how I was treated, how they embarrassed me." I know that I had to get over how my father left me and left my mom or I was going nowhere fast. I had to forgive my father for walking out and leaving my mom—a single mom—to raise two kids.

Romans 5:5 says that the love of God is shed abroad in my heart by the Holy Ghost. If God can shed love in my heart, God can also shed forgiveness in my heart. It's a matter of yielding. It is so imperative that you are released, and the Holy Ghost sheds that forgiveness in your heart. If I tell God, "I yield, I give myself to you. I need forgiveness placed in my heart. God, I can't forgive within my own ability and my own power, but I'm yielding myself as a vessel to you. God, will you place forgiveness in my heart?" Then, you'll be released from those who trespassed against you. God will release you from those who put things contrary to His Word in your life, knowingly or unknowingly. The enemy used many people that don't even know they were being used to try and make you captive. You can be free from it.

Knowing the Value of Money

Once you can perceive your vision and realize that God desires you to prosper, then next you must value the revelation of God. You have to value it; you have to respect it. The emotional ties to money in your life are important. You attract what you respect in life. Do you value money? I know it sounds strange, but money is attracted to people who are respectful of it and respectful of receiving it.

The problem is not a money problem. The deeper issue is that if you don't get to the root of it, you can never bring real healing and real wholeness. You have to identify, "How do I feel about money?" So many people don't even see the need to talk about it, but I ask you how you feel about it, because it is imperative.

Your checkbook or your wallet contains your money and where you hold your checks or your credit cards. If your cash, your checks, or your credit cards have value or importance in your life, you place them in a neat and orderly fashion. You make sure your cash is tucked away neatly. Your cards are in order, so you know where they are. Your checks have a ledger that you fill out to maintain order.

If your checkbook doesn't have a proper date, check number, who you wrote it to, an amount, a balance, you don't respect it. Are your credit cards mismanaged, with you not knowing what's in your wallet? Do you have three outdated cards that you should have cut up years ago, because they're expired? If this is the case–you don't respect them.

If all you have is $3, put it in a money clip. If you can honor three dollars, God can trust you with $3,000. If God can trust you with $3,000, he can trust you with $3,000,000 and so on. Order is the accurate arrangement of things. Without accurate arrangement, you have no authority in your life. What you don't respect in your life, you won't attract.

This is important, because the same is true about the anointing. If you don't recognize the anointing, the presence of God, if you don't know how to handle it, you won't attract it in your life. If you respect the Spirit of God, then you will attract the manifestation of His power in your life.

If you can't honor your husband, if you yell at him every single night, and you don't respect him, then he's not going to keep coming back. Some of you get familiar with people in your life, then you lose respect for them, and that's the most dangerous thing you can ever do. You must always respect the position God placed that person is in.

My husband is in a higher position of authority than me, because God placed him as the high priest of my household. Whether I like what he's doing at the time or not, as far as his personality, I've always been in love with Pastor Randy and always liked him. Do you know the reason I have? It's because I have a deep respect for him. I respect the position that God has placed him in and give him enough freedom to be the man that God has called him to be. I don't try to control him and make him avoid what God's called him to be, a man.

Governed by Your Words

There are words of poverty, and there are words of wealth. Your words will create the world you live in. The Bible says in Hebrews, Chapter 11:3 that God created the world by His Word. If He created the world with His spoken Word, you will create the world you live in by the words you speak. If you always use negative wording like, "I can't, I'll never, we won't, and we can't afford it," then you have eliminated God's ability to move on your behalf. You have eliminated all possibility.

You go to a grocery store, your son says, "I want this ice cream bar," and you say, "We can't afford that," you have missed an opportunity to teach him something. What you should have done is made him think by saying, "How can we afford that?" By putting in the word "how" you open up the possibility for God to move on your behalf.

You can be at the right place at the right time and meet the right person to enable a half a million dollars to flow into your life. That person may be one step down while you're turning down the aisle to check out your groceries. God can do it just like that. But the moment you say, "We can't," you eliminate all possibility of Him moving on your behalf, and you force down the function of that child's thinking.

You've got to use your mind, because all things are possible through Christ Jesus. Take off the limitations. Just because it doesn't happen this way doesn't mean it can't happen that way. Allow God to be God and move whatever way He wants, because He will defy natural laws. He'll walk on water to get to you. He'll speak to your problems, and the problems will be moved in your life. God will defy nature. He'll defy laws that would hold you back. He'll command obstacles that would hinder you to be removed in your life. He'll give you access to places that have been inaccessible to you.

You've got to allow God's power to be released and to move in your life by your words. That's why you've got to say, "How can we, we can do this, all things are possible, I will, and I'm learning to." You've got to discipline your mouth. In Proverb 18:21, the Bible says there is the power of life, and there is the power of death in the tongue. The Hebrew word for death means destruction.[1] Go to your Bible and pull up everything God has to say about the tongue, because your life is in there, and your destruction is in there. That's why Proverb 6:2 says you are snared by the words of your own mouth. Nobody else can stop God's destiny in your life. You set your own trap by what you speak.

That's why I've chosen to keep my mouth shut. If it's not edifying, if it's not encouraging, if it's not uplifting, it's not going to come forth out of my mouth. Everything that comes forth is going to be edifying and encouraging, according to the Word of God. I'm going to speak myself in psalms and hymns and make a melody in my own heart. I'm going to edify myself and nurture my soul with the Word of God.

The Bible says in Proverb 15:2, "The tongue of the wise useth knowledge aright: but the mouth of fools poureth out foolishness." When you talk foolishness, such as, "I can't," and "We won't be able to afford that," then the Bible says you are a fool, and out of your mouth you are pouring foolishness. This is because you are stopping what God wants to do in your life. So, learn to control your mouth. The Bible says in James 3:5 the man who cannot control his own tongue cannot control anything. How can you do great and mighty things if you can't tame your tongue? The Bible says your whole religion is in vain if you cannot control your mouth.

In Numbers 14:28, God says, "Tell them as surely as they have spoken it, it has come before my ears, and so shall I perform it." In other words, God does what you speak. As you speak it, He will move on your behalf. That's why when you understand to speak the Word of God, the Word of God cannot return void in your life.

That's why you've got to keep it before you. That's why you've got to meditate on it and bind it upon your heart. Put it upon your hand. Put it upon your children. Put Scripture on your refrigerator. Put them on your dresser drawers. Put them on the mirror. Post the Word of God. Listen to the Word of God over and over and over.

God's Word says, "Faith cometh by hearing, and hearing by the Word of God." (Rom. 10:17.) Without faith, it is impossible to please God. (Heb. 11:6.) You can't just think it; you've got to speak it. Your wealth or your poverty are within your words. This is a critical lesson to learn.

Proverb 21:23 says, "Whoso keepeth his mouth and his tongue keepeth his soul from troubles." So, if you can keep your mouth and keep your tongue, then you can keep your soul from trouble. Remember, God wants to prosper your soul, and your life should be a reflection of the prosperity of your soul. So, if you can keep your mouth, you can keep your soul from trouble.

You've got to tell yourself to shut up sometimes. Unless it edifies, unless it is encouraging, don't say it. Before you say anything, you've got to ask yourself this question, "Are my words in alignment with God's will?" Discipline yourself to do this before you say anything.

You need some mentors around you, so when you start speaking negativity, they don't feed on that, but they prevent you from falling. These are people that love you enough to say something about it. Let's face it, we all have bad days; and sometimes, we all start out by talking negatively and critically. You need people in your life to say, "No, stop it, that's enough."

Over the years, Pastor Randy has had to shut me up on more than one occasion. He would say gently but firmly, "Paula, I don't want to hear it." And, I would go pray, and recognize that he was right. My words have life, and my words have death. I'll wait until I get the victory, and I'll just keep my mouth shut until I can say something that edifies and encourages and uplifts.

Know Who You Are

When you undervalue who you are, the world will undervalue what you do. You can only overcome your condition by your position in Christ. This will continue until you recognize who you are–an heir of God, a joint heir of Christ. (Rom. 8:17.) You are an ambassador of God, which means you are a delegated representative of another kingdom.

If you undervalue yourself, then people will undervalue what you do. In other words, you cannot feel poor and undeserving and expect the blessing of God to overtake you. You can't do it. With a poor attitude and negative confession you will never change your condition. When we go into the inner city without ministry programs, we say, "It's one thing to be poor. It's another thing to feel poor." If you feel poor, if you feel unworthy, if you feel shameful, then you can't expect the blessing of God to overtake you.

You must become so certain of God's promises in your life. You have to know Deuteronomy 8:18 has your name on it. I say it like this, "God has given Paula White the power to get wealth." You've got to know that Deuteronomy 28:13 has your name on it, that God has made you the head and not the tail, that you shall not be beneath but you shall be above. You've got to know that

44

the Word of God declares you're going to be blessed coming in, and you're going to be blessed going out. You have to know the blessing of God is going to overtake you. You have to know that Psalm 115:13-14 say those that fear the Lord shall increase, they and their seed shall increase. You have to know God says that He has a prosperous way for you, which the course of life He has for you is higher than the course of life you have for yourself.

You have to know, "That is my promise. That word was written to me, Paula White." Until you see them manifest in your life, do not settle for anything less. Fight for the Word, because the Word has to work in your life. Heaven and earth shall pass away, but the Word will remain. (Matt. 24:35.) Like money, if you don't value yourself, nobody else will value you.

Some of you go into the office, and hang your head down when they call you in to talk to you about a raise. You might think you're worth ten dollars an hour, but they think you're worth twenty dollars an hour. And if they call you in and they say, "What do you think you should be paid?" and you say ten dollars, you undervalued yourself.

Walk without a spirit of timidity, because God has not given you the spirit of fear, but He's given you love, power and a sound mind. (2 Tim. 1:7.) If you're confident, it will say a lot about you. It goes back to value. It's not about you; it's about the God inside of you.

The way that you value yourself is determined by your knowledge of who is on the inside of you. The Bible says that I am the "temple of the Holy Spirit." (NIV, 1 Cor. 6:19.) I'm a house for God. I am the dwelling place for His presence. So, when I walk in and do my business, I'm doing God's business, because I am a sanctuary, a dwelling place, and the temple of God.

That's why I am confident to believe that supernatural wisdom can flow out of my mouth. James 1:5 says, "If anyone lack wisdom, let him ask of God." Wisdom is not knowledge. Knowledge is learned by works. Wisdom comes from God. It says that if anyone asks Him, God will give wisdom liberally and abundantly. Before I do any business in my daily routine, I ask God to give me wisdom.

I've watched God open my mouth when I didn't know what I was going to say. He'll do the same for you. He'll open your mouth, and He'll fill it, and you won't even have to take thought of what you're going to say. He'll fill it with the power of His wisdom and the power of His Word; and the power of the Holy Spirit will speak through you. We serve a supernatural God.

You have to begin to value yourself. You send signals, verbally and nonverbally, regarding how you value yourself. The Bible says mans looks on the outward appearance; God looks on the heart. (1 Sam. 16:7.) First impression is everything when you go in—how you dress, how you carry yourself, how you sit, and these are all nonverbal. When I had to shop at a thrift store for four years of my life, I believed God to give me the best looking dress in that thrift store. I'm telling you, we didn't have a dime, didn't have a dollar, but I still took time to look like an ambassador of God. Do the best with what you have in your present season. How you carry yourself now will determine what you look like in the future.

Using Money Wisely

Learn to make your money work for you. There are three ways: work hard; either receive an inheritance or win the lottery, some type of gifting; or investments, which have compounded interest working for you. Now, most of us will work hard, but this is not enough to live a complete life. We know this, because Florida is a state of retirees, and most of these retirees live beneath the poverty level because they didn't know how to make their money work for them.

Let the money you work for begin to earn money for you. Deut. 15:6 says, "You will lend and not borrow." How in the world do you think they're building those huge bank buildings downtown? How in the world do you think they're building those high rises? Your money is working for them.

You have to sacrifice now to give yourself a future. This is why you have to identify how you feel about money, because if you don't, you will never learn how to sacrifice. If you don't feel good about yourself, you will go thousands of dollars in debt to look nice, because you've got to have a dress to make you feel good. Well, that dress is going to be old in 2 weeks, and once you put $100 on your credit card, you'll spend $249 for it.

I heard someone say that the average family carries $8,000 of debt on their credit card. If that is true, then with the way the national interest is right now, it would take an entire lifetime of minimum payments to pay off $8,000 worth of debt. So, in other words, if you charge up $8,000, and you pay minimum payments, it's going to take you your full lifetime to pay off that debt.

Let me give you something else how to make your money work for you. If you are under 25, I can help you have a great future. Save $100 a month, $1,200 a year, at an average interest per annum–which right now, it's low, but in a few years it will bounce back up. Some years are going to be 18 percent, some years are going to be 6 percent, some years are going to be 4, some years 28 percent–but on average, by the time you retire at 65 years old, you'll have right at $1,000,000.

Then, when you're 65 years old, you're not worried, and you're not full of fear and anxiety about what happens to the government or what doesn't happen, or what happens here or what doesn't happen here. You've believed in yourself and you've disciplined yourself

If you want your money to take care of you, you must take care of it. You've got to learn to invest wisely. Don't ever go into business with a non-tither. If they rob from God, they're going to rob from you. If they steal from God, you better believe they are ultimately going to steal from you. Don't invest a day, don't invest a month, and don't invest a year with them.

When placing people in leadership, make sure they are tithers. The sheep of this ministry are way too precious to have any kind of thief in leadership. If they'll rob from God, they'll certainly rob from you. They'll rob from you spiritually, they'll rob from you emotionally, and they'll rob from you every other way. So, that's why you need to reconsider before you go into business with a non-tither. Don't waste years of you're life expecting a blessing if your in business or partnership with someone who is already cursed. (Mal. 3:8,9.) That's a "no-brainer."

Wise as Serpents, Gentle as Doves

The next thing you have to do is educate yourself. Most people don't know much about financial matters: simple things like how to handle money, how to budget, and how to manage. You should find out what the abbreviation IRA stand for, how do the Dow Jones operates, how to balance a ledger, and how to manage things in your life to take care of your family after you're gone. The Bible has much to say about these matters.

As I conclude this chapter, here are some final thoughts to guarantee success in supernatural living. They pertain to your character. Don't ever invest with anybody that doesn't have character. Because we are talking about taking care of your money, you should realize that if money has a value, so does the person who is holding it. Don't ever let anybody take care of your money that doesn't have character. With every investor that I've ever worked with, I know where he or she invests their money, how much money they have, and what they do with it. What they do with their money is what they're going to do with mine.

Character is character. Jeremiah 13:23 says, "Can an Ethiopian change his skin color, or can a leper his spots?" Can an evil man with an evil heart change his ways? Absolutely not. Character is character. Right is right, and wrong is wrong. You better find somebody that knows how to walk in character and integrity. Find out what they did with their money. Find out how they handle their affairs. I'll say it again: character is character. Don't let them get near your money if they don't have character. If they don't take care of themselves, they aren't going to take care of you. If they don't take care of those that they are supposed to and obligated to, they won't take care of you.

Don't ever marry a man that doesn't take care of his mother. Don't ever marry a woman that doesn't take care of people properly and treat people properly. If they'll yell at their mom, then they'll do it to you. Don't deceive yourself. You need to know those who labor among you. You need to know those you get into business with. You need to know those you minister with, because character is character, and it changes not.

You'd better find yourself a Joseph who won't compromise on morality, who won't compromise on principle, who will do the right thing when nobody else is looking. Find someone who will always walk in integrity, who will walk in honor, who will walk in principles. God will honor and raise that person up. And who shall stand before the holy hill of the Lord? Only those with clean hands and pure hearts.

I won't knowingly align myself with you if you don't have clean hands and a pure heart, because you will take me down. And, I'm not going to waste precious years aligned with you, if you don't have clean hands and a pure heart. I want to know your perception. I want to see how you treat people. Be careful before your go into covenant with anybody who doesn't walk in character and in the power of God.

Everything God told you to do, He not only will qualify you to do, but He also will equip you to do. But if you align yourself with people who are not in covenant with God, then they will pull you away from your vision. The enemy will attempt to use anything he can against you—your past, your hurt, your failures, and your flesh—to disqualify you as a candidate for supernatural living.

Once you perceive your vision and realize that God desires you to prosper, then you will value revelation. If you don't value revelation, then you will never respect the anointing. If you don't know how to respond to revelation, the anointing and the purpose of God, then money will not come to you. It is after you discover your destiny that you attract those things in your life, which are necessary to fulfill God's calling. What you respect in life, you attract. If you respect the Spirit of God, then you will attract the manifestation of His power in your life. For every vision, there is provision attached to it.

You are an ambassador of God, which means you are a delegated representative of another kingdom. So don't undervalue yourself or people will undervalue what you do. In other words, you cannot feel undeserving and expect the blessing of God to overtake you.

Chapter Five

THE PRINCIPLES
of COVENANT

Delegated Authority

omans 10:8,9 say, "That if thou shalt con-
fess with thy mouth the Lord Jesus Christ, and that
believe in thine heart that God hath raised him from the
dead, you will be saved." With your mouth, you use your
authority for salvation, deliverance, and healing. We
have authority by the covenant that God made with us. It
is through your relationship with God that you exercise
anointing.

It is important that we know this because when the
enemy comes at you and attacks your family—get a revelation. "For me and my house, we will be the head of
the house" (Josh. 24:15). If you are a parent, you have
delegated authority in your home to protect your children
and keep the devil on the run. You are to speak blessing
over your family to cover them against the schemes of
Satan. Your covenant with Jesus through the provision of
the Father, gives you access to His power.

After you have become a child of God, then you are
to become His disciple. Jesus delegated His authority to

his disciples. His disciples learned about the anointing through Jesus teaching and they put it into practice.

"If ye continue [if you remain] in my word, then ye are my disciples indeed" (John 8:31). The word disciple in Greek means "a pupil or learner." A disciple was not only a pupil, but also adherent; hence, they are spoken of as imitators of their teacher.[1]

Jesus delegated His authority to His disciples, and they learned about the anointing through His teaching— so, they could put into practice. Jesus said, "If ye continue [if you remain] in my word, then ye are my disciples indeed." (John 8:31, emphasis mine.) To those who have a relationship with God, He says if you continue, you are my disciples. The Greek word for continue means "to stay, to abide, to dwell, to endure, and to remain."[2] To continue does not mean, "I get a revelation, I see if it works, and if it doesn't come to pass in six months, I go on to the next revelation."

It's your word–if you continue, if you remain, if you dwell, if you endure, you can stand. In other words, to continue is not, "Let's see if this works, then I'll decide if I want to do it." To continue means, "I've got a Word, and I'm going to stand on it. I'm planted in the Word, so come hell or high water, my situations and circumstances will not dictate what I feel. The Word is the ultimate law, which I live by."

Covenant of Relationship

Jesus continued saying, "And ye shall know the truth, and the truth shall make you free" (John 8:32). You should know the truth. What truth? It is the truth of the

Word. Jesus said you shall know the truth. The Greek word for know is ginosko.[3] Ginosko signifies to be taking in knowledge, to come to know, recognize, understand, or to understand completely. In the New Testament, ginosko frequently indicates a relation between the person knowing and the object known. In other words, what is known is of value or importance to the one who knows and, hence, the establishment of the relationship. The verb is also used to convey the thought of connection or union, as between man and woman.[4] (Matt. 1:25, Luke 1:34.)

Therefore, it's not a knowledge based upon your intellect, but knowledge based upon the intimacy of an experience. Its Hebrew counterpart, to know, is the word yada, "Adam knew Eve his wife; and she conceived." (Genesis 4:1, emphasis mine.) [5] So when Jesus was saying, "you shall know the truth," He did not mean head knowledge, but rather, that you shall intimately be acquainted with the truth. That truth which you know shall set you free. We can establish that, through relationship, we are positioned for covenant.

In other words, the truth that I am intimately acquainted with will bring me into liberation, will bring me into freedom, will bring me out of bondage, and will bring me into deliverance, through Christ Jesus. So, how do I begin to walk out what God has promised me and take possession of what He's predestined for me? You have to know the Word. You can't just have knowledge. You can't go into the promises just because you can quote 100 Scriptures. It's not the ability to quote Scriptures. It's through knowing or being intimate with the Word. That Word which I am intimate with, that Word which has been birthed in the womb of my spirit.

First, it will deliver me, then it will free me, and then it will liberate me.

The Good Life

In John 10:10, Jesus gave His mission statement and purpose for coming to the world. He says, "I am come that they [my body, my children] might have life and have it more abundantly." (Emphasis mine.) The Amplified Bible says, "I came that they may have and enjoy life, and have it in abundance—to the full, till it." Jesus did not just come to earth to get you to heaven. He said, "I have come for you to have life and that you would enjoy life to its fullest."

My emphasis here is not to deny the existence of heaven, its reality, or its significance. I am, rather, trying to reveal that Jesus put His focus on what the kingdom of God was here on earth and what benefits it bestowed in the earth. Jesus told His disciples that, "There is no man that hath left house, or brethren, or sisters, or father, or mother, or wife, or children, or lands, for my sake, and the gospel's, but he shall receive an hundredfold now in this time ... and in the world to come eternal life." (Mark 10:29,30.)

Jesus also said, "Thy kingdom come. Thy will be done in earth, as it is in heaven" (Matt. 6:10). The kingdom is not future alone, but is now! We are to have what is in heaven here in the earth now! In other words, He said, "I want you to have my joy. I want you to have the peace of God. I want you to have prosperity."

And prosperity is not just about money. Prosperity means; welfare, well-being; affluence (wealth); success;

thrift, roaring trade; good fortune, smiles of fortune; blessings, and a godsend.⁶ I understand it to mean, to be profitable, to make advancement, and to have goodness in your life. God wants your relationships to be blessed and your household to be restored. Jesus said, "I come that you would have abundant life, that you would enjoy life." He didn't say, "You have to wait to get to heaven before you will be blessed."

God came to give me abundant life. He came to give me abundant life. What it means me is to be emotionally stable, spiritually stable, physically healed, financially whole, and prosperous, family intact. How do I begin to live the abundant life of Christ?

You cannot walk in unforgiveness and have God's breakthrough. You cannot be a non-tither and have God's breakthrough. You cannot be sleeping in another bed besides the marriage bed and have God's breakthrough. It takes all that we've learned to build it and process it to go into the place that God has for us.

Do you want to break through to the promises of God? Are you going to just live in a sick, broke, and disgusted state? Are you sick and tired of being sick and tired? Are you ready to take possession of what God's promised? Do you want continual joy flowing in your life? Do you want peace in your household? Do you want provision? Are you tired of scraping from the bottom of the barrel? What will it take for you to receive the abundant life? It is found in covenant. A covenant based upon the principles of Gods economy not the worlds.

You are not product of or bound to the world's system. That's why it doesn't matter what happens to the economy, what happens at your job, what happens in your neighborhood, what happens in your city, where you live, or the nation of America. You're not a product of the world's system but of the kingdom of God. Therefore, you don't operate on the same principles that the world operates on.

Covenant 101

God's Words are covenant. It is a legally binding contract between God and man. A covenant is an agreement or pact between two or more parties. It is an agreement or a pact between two or more parties to carry out the terms that are agreed upon.[7]   If this is a covenant, a legally binding contract, there are two questions I have to ask you. First, "Did you know that God is a covenant keeper?" Second, "Are you, as a Christian, in covenant relationship with Jesus?" This is important, because everything you need is in covenant. All God's benefits of the blessing, such as, healing, deliverance, salvation, financial increase, wholeness, and fulfillment are available because of covenant. What we receive from God is not because of you; it is for you. It is not because you pray 39 hours or because you don't pray 39 hours. It is because of covenant. It doesn't matter what you do or what you don't do. It's not because of your works or your righteousness. It's because of covenant.

You can have somebody who's been pure, like little saint Suzie ("Miss goodie two shoes" all her life) or somebody who's been impure, like Sandy, the sinner, all her life. (It doesn't matter.) God will raise both of them up. God may release Sandy, the sinner, into greatness. Suzie, the saint, never get anywhere—if she thinks it is because of her works and her doing good that she is blessed.

It has nothing to do with that. You are justified because of covenant. You are sanctified because of covenant. It also has to do with covenant that you are sanctified. It has to do with covenant that you are saved, and you receive covenant by faith. The salvation I received is because of covenant. The justification I received is because of covenant. Everything is based upon covenant.

My children will be saved because of covenant, not because I raised them perfectly. It wasn't because I knew how to dot every "i" and cross every "t" perfectly. It's because of covenant. It's covenant that says, "Train up a child in the way he should go, and when he is old, he will not depart from it" (Prov. 22:6).

My husband will rise up and call me blessed in the gates of the city because of covenant. (Prov. 31:23.) My seed shall possess the gates of my enemy because of covenant. (Prov.31:31.) I'll be the head and not the tail because of covenant. (Deut. 28:13.) I'll be blessed going in and coming out because of covenant. (Deut. 28:6.) Everything that I put my hand to shall prosper because of covenant. (Deut. 28:8.) Wherever my feet go, God will give it to me because of covenant. (Josh. 1:3.) No weapon formed against me shall prosper because of covenant. (Isa. 57:14.) A thousand are going to fall at my side, and ten thousand are going to fall at my right hand, but it will not come nigh me because of covenant. (Ps. 91:7.) When the enemy comes in like a flood, God has raised up a standard against him because of covenant. (Isa. 59:19.)

Covenant, everything you need is in covenant, everything. If you don't understand this, you'll never be able to possess what God's promised you. Good people, people who love God, are destroyed for lack of knowledge. (Hos. 4:6.) They know there is a covenant, but they don't understand how to operate in or process the covenant. We are receiving God's promises by the covenant, and we activate the blessing of God through our faith in the covenant.

If I am a Christian and am I want to be in a covenant relationship, I have to ask myself this, "What kind of covenant am I to enter into? What does my covenant with God look like? What is the pattern? What are the rights of it? What are the contingencies? What does this covenant, this legally binding contract, say to my life?"

The Abrahamic Covenant

There are several different types of covenants in the Word. There's the Noachian Covenant, the Adamic Covenant, the Edenic Covenant, the Abrahamic Covenant, and then there is the New Covenant. As a New Testament believer, Jesus Christ has brought me into covenant. So, what does the covenant look like? What are the rights that I have? The Book of Hebrews, specifically chapters 5 through chapter 7, give a pattern, or tell us that we are the fulfillment of the type of the Abrahamic Covenant. The Abrahamic Covenant is an eternal covenant. It's very important that you understand that. It means that it goes forever and ever and ever. The New Testament is patterned similar to the Abrahamic Covenant.

When God called Abraham (Genesis 12), the first thing He said to him was, "I will make of thee a great nation." In other words, "I'm going to make your people great." Well, this is good news, because you may have come from some crazy background. God was saying, "I'm about to clean up all the messed up people and make them a nation. I'm going to sanctify them, and I'm going to make your people great." In other words, what once worked for a bunch of heathens, drinking whiskey, like freaky Freddy folly in his sin, are now about to become saved, sanctified, and filled with the Holy Ghost. "I'm going to make your people great."

Next God said, "I will bless you." When you need to get in the Word and find out what blessing means. Both Hebrew and Greek define blessing "to bestow prosperity and goodness, to worship God as good, to receive His goodness, and announce it to others, the prosperity or happiness resulting from such bestowal."[8] Blessing is the empowerment to succeed and prosper. In other words, God says, "I am going to empower you to succeed and to prosper. I will give you the goods on the inside of you that will enable you to manifest anything on the outside. I will empower you to succeed and to prosper, to be advanced, to be profitable, to be good."

That's why you can put me in Haiti, and I'll prosper. You can put me in Africa, and I'll prosper. You can put me in Tampa, Florida, and I'll prosper. Put me in a church with only 20 people, and it will prosper. Put me in a church with 2,000, and it will prosper. It is because it is nothing external. It is internal. It is because I recognize, according to 2 Corinthians, "But we have this treasure [deposit of wealth] in earthen vessels, that the excellency of the power may be of God, and not of us"

(4:7, emphasis mine). There is power inside of you that is greater than anything on the outside of you. That's why He said, "Greater is he that is in you, than he that is in the world" (1 John 4:4). If He is in me, then I am blessed—empowered to prosper and to succeed.

You cannot be looking to everything externally to make it. It's not an external thing but internal. You are not contingent upon the economy. Let the Dow go up or go down it does not change God's Word or plan. Let the NASDAQ fall or the yen drop, it doesn't matter. God is not dependent upon external circumstances to guarantee our success.

That's why Isaac could go into a land of famine, sow his seed, and reap a hundredfold harvest. (Gen. 26:12.) He was blessed—empowered to succeed and to prosper. That' why Joshua 1:8 says to meditate on the Word, and then, God will make your way prosperous.

Do you want to possess what God promised you? Do you want to walk in the covenant blessing? You need to believe that God wants you blessed. God intended you to be empowered to prosper and succeed. What some people call blessings are what I call the fringe benefits: cars, homes, clothes, and whatever "floats your boat." They are not the blessing. The blessing is the empowerment to prosper and to succeed, based upon the power on the inside of you!

God was saying to Abraham, and is now saying to his descendants (Gal. 3:26), "I will make thy name great." (Gen. 12:2.) In other words, you're going to become important. It literally means, "That Abraham will acquire fame but also that he will be highly esteemed as a man of superior character."[9] The Bible says that nothing is higher than a good name (Prov.

22:1). God can make your name great.

How does God take someone like me—a messed up Mississippi girl, who was sexually and physically abused; whose dad committed suicide at five years old; came out of poverty, lived in a trailer—and raise her up to go to the White House and to stand before kings and queens, to eat dinner with President George W. Bush, Prime Minister Benjamin Netanyahu, General Colin Powell, and Lady Margaret Thatcher? It's because God said it in His word, and I have appropriated it. "I'll make your name great. I'll put you in places you could never put yourself. I'll open doors that money made will never open for you, because I will make your name great."

God continues when He said, "Thou shalt be a blessing" (Gen. 12:2). Now, you can't be a blessing until you've been blessed. God was saying, "It's not just for you, but you're going to have a sphere of influence so that everyone around you is going to be blessed because you're in their lives."

Genesis 12:3 says, "I will bless them that bless thee." Everyone who blesses me, that discerns the gift, the call, and the anointing that is upon my life, man, if they even get me a cup of cold water, they're blessed. If they open a door, they're blessed. I'm not talking about people who know me. I'm talking about the stranger in the mall who opens the door. They don't even know they just got the blessing of the Lord. God is saying, "I bless everybody who blesses you."

The Scriptures continue by telling us, "And I'll curse everybody that curses thee." God says, "I'll mess with those that mess with you." That's why you're not going to have to fight your battles, "because vengeance is mine … saith the Lord" (Rom. 12:19). The battle is not yours.

You're not going to have to battle in the boardroom. You're not going to have to battle in any room. God says, "I will fight your battle. I will take vengeance. I am a righteous God. My name is Elohim, the Supreme One, and the Righteous Judge. And then He goes on in Genesis 12:3 and He says, "All the families of the earth shall be blessed." Your community's going to be blessed because you're living there.

When we moved to Florida, the place where we living was falling apart all around us. We moved into a 2 bedroom, 1 bath—small home—and there was a warlock right next to us whose house was all shabby, weeds growing up. The person on the other side was an alcoholic. The house was all dingy, dank, messed up, and everything else you can imagine. After we moved in, we began to claim our land blessed, and within one year, the cultic neighbor moved out. Their house began to prosper. The next person moved out, and that house began to prosper.

There was a shack falling apart across the street. They tore it down and built two-story buildings. I'm telling you, our property value went from $80,000 to almost $300,000 in just a few short years. Why? It's because God says, "I will bless everything around you." That's why. People want you to move into their neighborhood, because you become a blessing in that neighborhood. They're blessed, simply because you're living there and you're in covenant.

God will give you perception and ability to see a thing other people can't see. Here is where the covenant of God begins to release. It is when you realize that He wants to reach out to those who do not know Him. As He blesses you, in turn, He blesses others. As He blesses you others recognize that the "hand of God" is upon your life. (Ezra 7:9.) They see that favor has made its dwelling place in your house (Ex. 12:36.)

The promise of prosperity is defined in the Abrahamic covenant and is well demonstrated in the life of Abraham, and his sons, Isaac, and Jacob. God made Abraham rich to accomplish the task that was destined in his life. Each of his sons prospered according to the destiny of their lives. Each of Abraham's sons gave God credit for their achievements and accomplishments due to the covenant God initiated with Abraham, the father of faith. Likewise we have access to the Abrahamic covenant through Abraham's son, Jesus. (Matt. 1:17).

Now we who are children of God are also children of Abraham and are blessed by his covenant with God. (Gal. 3:9.) The blessings of Abraham have come to the Gentiles (nations and ethnic people groups who are not Jewish) through Jesus Christ. (Gal.3:14.) But the ways we receive our blessing are through spiritual and generational inheritance. In other words, the promises of the covenant were made to Abraham and his seed (descendants). But Paul, the apostle, makes a startling revelation. He says that the promises were not "to seeds, as of many; but as of one, and to thy seed, which is Christ." (Gal. 3:16.)

You see, the promises are not deposited or transferred by the law. "For if the inheritance be of the law, it is no more of promise: but God gave it to Abraham by promise [covenant]." (Gal. 3:18, emphasis mine.) This means that covenant, eternal covenant, is a binding contract. The contract made with Abraham was made to him and his descendants. "And if ye be Christ's, then are ye Abraham's seed, and heirs according to the promise"

(Gal. 3:29). Our blessing is contingent upon our faith but made possible and provisional by the covenant of God with Abraham. The sacrifice of Christ's blood bound this contract. Through Him we have life, abundant life—and we are empowered to prosper and succeed.

Chapter Six

THE COVENANT
of TITHING

The Prosperity Perspective

$\mathcal{I}$ want to continue on the subject of covenant, going deeper into its meaning by laying a foundation of truth so that you can receive this teaching God gave me. God transformed my mindset concerning prosperity, and it has changed my life. But before we continue on to covenant, let's visit the subject of prosperity again and make it plain. Prosperity to his servants is more than money. Money is only a fringe benefit. Prosperity is not like a currency exchange program God has set up. At a currency exchange booth at an International airport, you can change your American dollar bills into Yen, Euro, or some other foreign currency. It is not a "scratch my back, I'll scratch your back" policy. Your seed does not move God. He is moved by your obedience. God does not repay us a return, like a broker through an investment plan with your IRA, annuity, 401k, or your capital investment plan. God responds to covenant.

Let me explain. God wants to be intimate with us. Your heavenly Father is more interested in you than your money. He is a jealous God. (Deut. 4:24.) Biblical prosperity is not money, but it does include monetary rewards. The riches in Christ Jesus begin with a relationship. Through our relationship with God, and discovering the meaning of covenant, we realize that God has a plan and a destiny for each and every one of us. Prosperity starts with intimacy, develops through relationship, and eventually matures into a lifestyle of worship. Prosperity is knowing who Christ is and who you are. How can you expect God to place thousands of dollars into your hands if you do not know what your purpose, destiny and function is in the kingdom?

We can discover God's methods for the prosperity perspective, which is demonstrated as our example throughout Abraham's journeys. God called Abraham to a land that he knew not from the city of Ur in Mesopotamia. (Acts 7:2.) It was there that Abraham dwelled in a highly developed city with brick multi-family units and elevated story buildings, used as high rises in the "downtown" metropolitan.[1] When Abraham took on a nomadic form of life, he would have turned his wealth into flocks and herds, so that his wealth could travel with him. (Gen.13:2.)[2]

It was in the town of Haran where Terah, Abraham's father, died at the age of 205 years old. (Gen. 11:32.) It was also where he inherited his father's material possessions. Haran was an important crossroads and commercial city in Syria.[3] Because of his father's death, it was time for Abraham to officially accept his new family responsibilities and to adjust from an urban-based existence to the constant travel of pastoral nomads. There were, no doubt, several barriers to face: language, social, economic, and being unfamiliar with Canaanite land laws, only to mention a few. But more importantly, as an immigrant, Abraham was constrained to obey the legal traditions of the people of Canaan.

According to most historians, nomads were not permitted to trade with local merchants without owning property.[4] Abraham never owned property until he purchased the cave of Machpelah as a burial site for his wife Sarah. (Gen. 23:9.) Another barrier is described with the stories of wells in Genesis 20 and 26. There, it tells us that there were specific zones designated for water use by urban-based communities. Within these zones, outsiders were seldom given water rights, especially if the village felt that the pastoral nomads were threatening the economic welfare. (Gen 26:20.) In that case, it was a certainty that the newcomers would be forced to leave.[5]

Abraham received his initial inheritance from his earthly father and started on his journey, but it was the heavenly Father who called Abraham and commissioned him with destiny and purpose. God alone was Abraham's source. (Gen. 14:23.) It was this high calling that motivated Abraham to leave a pagan lifestyle and surrender to Jehovah God. Abraham believed God and it was accredited unto him righteousness. (Gen. 15:6.) It was through faith, obedience, and relationship that Abraham trusted in his God. It was through intimacy and through this faith journey that he discovered principles for the prosperity perspective.

The prosperity of Abraham was not just the flocks; gold and silver. It was more than possessions. For "the Lord had blessed Abraham in all things" (Gen. 24:1, emphasis mine). Had the Lord not been watching over Abraham as his shield, and his exceeding great reward (Gen. 15:1), Abraham would have lost his flocks to a famine in Canaan (12:10), and lost his wife to Pharaoh in Egypt (12:17). He would have been over taken with bankruptcy by poor grazing conditions in undeveloped land (13:10-12), been defeated in war (14:13-16), and never inherited the land (23:15). He would have hopelessly remained childless (15:2), and would have never been able to offer up his son in worship (22:12).

Had it not been for the Lord, where would we be? Abraham learned that prosperity was more than riches. Without God, Abraham's wealth would not have been able to buy his way out of his challenges. It was the favor and the mercy of God that kept him to the end. This is the prosperity perspective—to recognize that without Him, without purpose, without destiny, without relationship, and without His blessing we are nothing! Abraham discovered that, through a covenant relationship with God, according to his calling and purpose—he was destined for greatness. This needs to be your goal— to find your purpose, destiny, and to fulfill His calling, through His prosperity.

Friend, I have researched and prepared background material to this extent to teach you an important principle. Abraham had a lot going for him, that is obvious, but without God's blessing, his prosperity could not have developed to its intended extent. The Biblical meaning of prosperity must be kept in its original perspective. How you view yourself, your calling and your purpose will determine if you will ever reach the level in God that He intends for you to reach. Where you are now is not where God sees you in the future, but your future prosperity depends upon today's perspective.

The Eternal Covenant

"And I [God] will establish my covenant between me and thee and thy seed after thee in their generations for an everlasting covenant, to be a God unto thee, and to thy seed after thee" (Genesis 17:7, emphasis mine). What exactly is God saying here? He's saying, "This covenant is not just for you, Abraham, but this covenant is for you and your seed forevermore." It's an eternal covenant. It is never ending.

But, you may ask, "What in the world does that have to do with me?" We discovered in chapter 5 that Galatians 3:29 says, "And if ye be Christ's, then are ye Abraham's seed, and heirs according to the promise." If ye be in Christ, the anointed One and His anointing, then you are the seed of Abraham and heirs to the promise.

Do you realize what that means? God said, "I wanted to give you a little glimpse of what was going to come for you. When I showed you this part of the covenant, I was simply giving you a foretaste of what I was going to bring in your life. Every promise I ever gave to Abraham is for you today. Everything I spoke to Abraham is for you today, because it's an eternal covenant."

But that's not all for you, because the author and writer of Hebrews says that the new covenant is based on better promises. (Heb. 8:6.) He said, "That was just the foundation. That was just a little glimpse. That's just a little bit. Allow me to say it like this: 'I'm getting ready to blow your mind.'" He said, "Now, I'm moving you into greater promises and greater covenant. This was the foundation, and if you don't understand that covenant, you won't understand this covenant."

"All the promises are for me. That's great, but I still don't get it, Paula. How does it happen?" I'm getting ready to tell you what He has promised you. You are blessed—empowered to prosper and succeed. Everywhere you go, you are going to be blessed. He's going to mess with those who mess with you. He's going to fight your battles. He's going to be your protector. He's going to be your shield. He's going to be your exceeding great reward. "Praise God, but How does it happen you may ask?"

The Tithe Principle

Here's how it works. A covenant is a process of exchange. Remember, covenant means an agreement or a pact between two parties. When Abraham was given this covenant, the Bible declares, in Genesis 14, verses 17 through 20, that he went and he paid tithes to Melchizedek.

Do you understand what a tithe is? Do you think it is 10 percent of your gross income? That's not what tithe is. I want to teach you the Word. Tithe is not intended that you focus on the 10 percent of your gross income. Many people love God, but they don't have information, and the Bible says without information and knowledge we perish. (Hosea 4:6.) It says, "With all your getting, get understanding." (Prov. 4:7.) The truth that you know, that you are intimately acquainted with, will bring you into deliverance, will bring you into freedom, will bring you into liberation. Your biggest enemy is not what you know; it's what you don't know.

Today is your day of deliverance, because the Bible

declares that the covenant was sealed when Abraham paid tithe of ALL unto Melchizedek. Tithe is not money. Tithe is your all. Don't miss this. If you miss this, you'll miss the transition that releases you into the covenant promises. Everything you need in your life is in the covenant. You receive it, by faith, through the covenant. Abraham paid tithes to Melchizedek. I will come back to this later in this chapter.

In other words, tithe became the covenant connector to the promises. Do you know why most people miss this? They think of money immediately, and that will mess with your mind. If there had been no tithe, there would be no blessing, and there would have been no receipt of the promise. Tithe, which was by faith, was what connected the covenant and set it into motion to operate. The Holy Ghost gave me this word so I can empower you to walk in the liberty, freedom, and the promises that God predestined for you. Tithe is the covenant connector to the promises.

Hebrews 5:6 says, "Thou art a priest for ever after the order of Melchisedec." He's talking about Jesus. You'll find it several times throughout the book of Hebrews. In other words, He's saying, "You are after the order or patterned after Melchisedec." The Abrahamic Covenant is a type and shadow of the New Covenant. So, if tithe was the covenant connector to the promise for Abraham, then tithe has to be the covenant connector to the promise for us.

If the tithe is the covenant connector, and the covenant has everything I need in life, what was the purpose of Jesus coming? His mission and purpose was to bring you the life that He desired for you to live more abundantly. (John 10:10.)

The first thing to know is this: tithing is redemptive. Notice that redemption is a covenant term. In Leviticus, in the New International Version, it says, "Nothing that a man owns and devotes to the Lord–whether man or animal or family land–may be sold or redeemed; everything so devoted is most holy to the Lord. No person devoted to destruction may be ransomed; he must be put to death" (Lev. 27:28, emphasis mine).

The Devoted, or First, Things

Let me draw your attention to the word devoted. It deals with first things. Devoted things and first things have the same meaning, and that meaning is irrevocable giving to God. When you give something to God, you cannot take it back. In other words, first things and devoted things are things that belong to God and to God only. Now, God said, "There are things I call devoted, there are things I call holy, there are things I call first things that belong to me and to me alone. They are mine." He lays claim to them.

Exodus 13 says, "The Lord said to Moses, 'Consecrate to me every firstborn male. The first offspring of every womb among the Israelites belongs to me, whether man or animal.' Then Moses said to the people, 'Commemorate this day, the day you came out of Egypt, out of the land of slavery, because the Lord brought you out of it with a mighty hand'" (13:1-3, NIV). It means that, "Whether it's a male son, whether it's an animal, whether it's fruit, or whether it's grain, all first things belong to me."

It is interesting to me that most of the people I've

either met or known who are in full-time ministry are firstborn children. The firstborn seems to have tremendous significance in understanding the principle of first things, because it has to do with redemption, which has to do with covenant.

Holy things or the devoted things are God's. Think of it this way, "I can't touch that." God sees the first thing, the first principle, as the root governing all the rest. In other words, the first thing is not how you look at it; it's how God sees it. It's what I call the principle of tithe or first things. So, first things represent more. They represent the total. It means whatever the first portion is used for determines what happens to the remaining portion.

If the part of the dough offered as first fruits is holy, then the whole batch is holy. "If the root is holy, so are the branches." (Romans 11:16.) Do you know what He said? He said, "A little leaven leaveneth the whole lump." He sees the root, the part, as the whole. It's an important principle.

The Bible declares "Do not hold back offerings from your granaries [or your vats.] You must give me the firstborn of your sons. Do the same with your cattle and your sheep. Let them stay with their mothers for seven days, but give them to me on the eighth day" (Exodus 22:29,30, NIV). When someone tithes, they are actually giving God the first fruits, or the first thing, or the first principle, or the devoted thing, or the holy thing. The tithe you bring to the Lord, it is holy. Give the first thing to God.

When thinking of a tithe, most people calculate a formula of 10 percent out of 100 of their gross income. But tithe is more than just 10 percent. "What do you mean, Paula?" I need to explain this so you can under-stand what this has to do with you walking in joy, peace, prosperity, and provision; or even putting diapers on your baby; and putting food on the table. "What in the world does this have to do with me?"

Presume we agreed that the tithe is the first tenth out of a percentage equal to a hundred, and you get paid weekly. Once you deposit your paycheck, you begin to write out bills: your gas bill, your phone bill, you write a check to Sears, or J.C. Penney's. Eventually, you'll use up all your money that you earned that week. You know you need to bring your tithe into the Lord. The second week, you come out with the mortgage due, and it eats up the whole check. And then the third week, you take your entire check, and you think you're bringing your tithe to the Lord, because it's the amount of ten percent each week.

But that's not the tithe. Tithe is the first tenth and the first tenth represents the whole. What you do if you write out the first check for something other than your tithe is you're giving to that cause (for an example, your gas bill). In essence, you are saying to the gas company, "I give you honor. I give you praise. I thank you gas company, for providing for my family. Thank you that you keep me warm. Thank you, that you heal my body. Thank you, AT&T. I'm so grateful that you can find my son when he's lost. AT&T, thank you that you can bring home my wayward husband. AT& T, I know you can reach all around the world, so AT&T, I worship you, because I make you first, and first things are holy things, devoted things."

What you plant first has nothing to do with your money. It has to do with covenant. What you give first sanctifies the rest. So therefore, you are saying, "Thank you, Ford Motor Company; I thank you, AT&T; I thank you, Sears"—because by paying that first with the tenth that was holy, you now sanctified all those other things as your God. Now, isn't that ridiculous? None of us would do that. "Paula, why do you have to get so technical, you must ask?"

We have established that God says, "Every first thing belongs to me." Why do you think Abraham had to bring Isaac? And He said, "Take now thy son, thy only son" (Gen. 22:2). Isaac wasn't his only son. He had Ishmael and six other sons by Keturah. (Gen. 25:1-3.) Isaac was first. Likewise, why did the Israelites go into Jericho and destroy Jericho first? It was because Jericho was the first place of battle after the Jordan River and before possessing Canaan land. It was the tithe. Tithe is not money but what is devoted to God of the first things. It's the first tenth, the first fruits, or the devoted things.

God says, "You have a male donkey, he's a firstborn. All first things belong to me" (see Exodus 13:11-16). We know some things are clean and some things are unclean. A donkey is without cloven hoofs and does not chew the cud, so it is unclean. God said, "You want to use that donkey. Okay, that's understandable; you need the donkey." And God's not going to say you can't use the donkey, but He'll say it's holy.

If you used an unclean animal, you would have to redeem it. How do you redeem it? By bringing a male lamb, that which is clean, and sacrificing it. When you redeem something, it must die. You're going to get all this in just a minute. And God said, "If you don't do that, it's better to break the neck of the donkey." In other words, God says, "Break the neck, destroy the thing that you're going to use—if you decide to use the first thing that's holy—because it is going to bring complete destruction in your life." He said, "It's better to just break its neck and destroy it than use it, if you haven't redeemed it."

"Pastor Paula, what does this have to do with me, walking in joy?" Well, I'm glad you want to know. Why does all this make a difference? It's because the tithe is redemptive, and by giving God the portion, the first portion, then you've redeemed the ninety percent that God said you can use however you want. So, the first thing determines how everything else will go. Say, "Covenant." So when you write your first check, you make sure, by faith, that it's a holy one, because it's the first thing. All right? Whatever thing or bill you pay first anoints the rest.

First Fruits

The literal meaning of tithe is a tenth.[6] But systematically, a tithe is a concept of giving—directly connected to the first fruits offering. This is much more than what we've been taught to believe. It's not just about bringing ten percent of our income into the house of the Lord. The tithe and the first fruits offering are similar, but where they are different is that the actual amount of the first fruits is nowhere stated in Scripture. It appears that its actual practice was a liberal offering that was brought forth abundantly by the people during times of revival and reformation. (2 Chron. 31:5.)

The first fruits offering was one of the feasts on the Jewish calendar that fell immediately following the

Passover. It was to be presented as a wave offering before the Lord. By this, acknowledgement was made that all came from God and belonged to Him. This example was to demonstrate "the bounteous harvest of grain or barley, which would eventually follow because of God's providence." [7]

Both the Old Testament and New Testament warrant out belief that the ceremonial presentation of the first fruits had, beyond its obvious implications, a typical and symbolical significance. Israel is spoken of as God's "first fruits," dedicated to Him. (Jer. 2:3.) Christ, in His resurrection, is "the firstfruits of them that slept" (1 Cor. 15:20). The festival "Feasts of the First Fruits" took place on the first day after the Passover Sabbath—the day Christ rose from the dead. (Mark 16:1-6.)

Consider Paul's thoughts on this subject in 1 Corinthians 15:23, "But every man in his own order: Christ the first fruits; afterward they that are Christ's at his coming." Who or what is the firstfruits? Christ is the firstfruit. Romans 8:29 says, "For whom he did fore-know, he also did predestinate to be conformed to the image of his Son, that he might be the firstborn among many brethren."

"What does all this mean, Paula?" Romans tells us that Jesus was the firstborn. First Corinthians declares Him to be the first fruit. Exodus says we are always to bring the first fruit. So we have established the firstborn, first fruit, first thing, devotion, and tithe all mean the same thing. So, if I translate that properly, 1 Corinthians 15:23 and Romans 8:29 declares that Jesus has now become my tithe, my devoted thing that makes the rest holy, because He is the first fruit. The emphasis here is on the first portion and not a tenth. The tithe is the connector to the covenant. I can't receive the covenant without Jesus, but Jesus is my first portion, my first fruit, or my tithe.

God wanted a family, He gave His Son. Christ redeemed us from the curse of the law by becoming the curse. (Gal. 3:13.) How did He accomplish this? He, the firstborn, the tithe, which Scriptures say belong to the Lord, accomplished this by being sacrificed. Remember, to redeem something, it has to die. That which is holy has to die to redeem that which is unholy, to purify and sanctify it. This allows you to walk in covenant. Before anybody was ever birthed into the kingdom of God, He redeemed the rest of the body from the curse. He became the righteousness of God so we may be righteous.

The first fruit or the tithe is redemptive. It's not about money its; about Jesus. He is your tithe. The tithe is what redeems us apart from the whole. When I bring my tithe, I connect to the covenant of Jesus Christ, then, by faith, I can receive every covenant blessing. I can walk in healing. I can walk in prosperity. I can walk in goodness. I can walk in mercy. I can walk in grace. I can walk in joy. This is because He paid the price for me.

The Covenant of the Tithe

Tithe is not just money, it's everything. It's redemption. It is the connector to the covenant promise. It's not a money issue we are dealing with; it's an obedience issue. So how do I walk in it? For tithing to work and have God's blessing, it must be done by faith. If we follow the letter of the law, and not the spirit of the law then tithing becomes a magical formula—available to anyone of any relation to participate in, regardless of their heart or faith. Before there was a law, instruction, or commandments on tithing, Abraham gave a tithe. Before there was ever a covenant with Abraham, he gave tithes. (Gen 14:20.) They were tithes of faith, obedience, and recognition unto God. He and He alone was Abraham's supplier. Therefore, Abraham received the promises and the inheritance of the promise through patience and faith (Heb. 6:12).

Tithing is not an Old Testament (covenant) principle. In fact, tithing was initiated before the law. But the New Covenant considers Christ a "first fruit." Abraham received the covenant by faith, and he received the benefits of it before Jesus consummated it. So how do you walk like Abraham to receive the same blessings? It begins with faith. "Without faith it is impossible to please him: for he that cometh, to God must believe that he is, and that he is a rewarder of those who diligently seek Him." (Hebrews 11:6.)

Probably the best explanation of tithe in the Bible is found in Malachi 3. "For I am the Lord, I change not; therefore, ye sons of Jacob are not consumed" (Malachi 3:6). That means Jesus Christ [is] same today, yesterday, and forever (Heb. 13:8). "Even from the days of your fathers ye are gone away from mine ordinances, and have not kept them" (Mal. 3:7a). Do you know what an ordinance is? It's a sacrament. It's the same as communion or a holy act in honor to God. "Return unto me, and I will return unto you, saith the Lord of hosts. But ye said, Wherein shall we return? Will a man rob God?" (Mal. 3:7b, 8a). The verb translated "rob" (Hebrew qaba) is rare in the Old testament. It is, although, quite heavily used in the Jewish writings of the law called the Mishnah and the Talmud. The use of qaba, "to rob," is well established in Talmudic literature to mean "to take forcibly".[8]

Therefore, in this context, we can safely say that robbing is different than stealing. Robbing can be defined as to defraud with the intention to bring harm, so if you rob, you bring physical harm to someone. If the tithe is separate and holy and is our covenant connector, when you take the tithe—the tithe of money, that which is holy—unto yourself and not unto God, you bring physical harm to the body of Christ.

Cursed with a Curse

"But ye say, 'Wherein have we robbed thee?' In tithes and offerings. Ye are cursed with a curse" (Mal 3:8b, 9a). "Cursed," and "curse" come from the same Hebrew root word, *arar. It comes from araru, a word based upon an Akkadian word, which was another dialect similar to Ancient Biblical Hebrew, well known during Old Testament times. In Akkadian, it meant "to snare, bind, noose, or sling." Therefore the Hebrew understanding means "to bind (with a spell), hem in with obstacles, render powerless to resist."[9]

To be cursed is to be rendered powerless, unable to perform tasks to their fullest potential, or to be road-blocked from your path or destiny. It literally means to invoke demonic principalities and powers. So, when you refuse to bring the first things to God–which is the only thing that has the power to redeem the rest–then you bring a curse or render yourself powerless. God does not need to curse you, for you curse yourself through your disobedience. You touched what was holy.

That's why when the Israelites went to Jericho, God said, "Don't touch it." They went to Jericho, and Achan took the sanctified thing, and 36 people had to die—because he touched what was holy. (Josh. 7:5.) It was the first fruit, the tithe, or, literally, the devoted, accursed things. To be cursed with a curse means that by withholding the tithe, the devoted things that are sacred, or holy, to God, everything else you have is cursed, unholy, polluted, or contaminated.

When we speak of the effects of withholding the devoted thing from God, we can compare the lives of Saul to David to see two drastic scenarios. Saul was not a (sexually) immoral king like most of the kings listed in Scripture. But when you look at King David, you see a man with the heart of God, who was a worshipper, and was one of the most righteous kings in Israel's history. But, David was a murderer, an adulterer and a liar. Saul had fits of rage, and on one occasion, was so desperate to get a word from the prophet Samuel, after he had died, that Saul dabbled into necromancy (a form of witchcraft that invokes the spirits of the dead).

Why was David allowed to remain as king when God rejected Saul? It was because God told Saul that they were to destroy a city, to destroy everything in it. Why? It was because the city was the tithe or devoted thing (literally, accursed). Samuel came to Saul and said, "What is this? I hear the bleating of sheep." (1 Sam. 15:14.) In other words, "You touched what was holy, and now I reject you, because you have removed yourself apart from the whole." He took what was holy and made it unclean. Remember, the Bible said it was better to break the neck of the donkey, because what you don't destroy will destroy you, if you don't make it holy and sanctify it.

When Saul was confronted by Samuel he said, "Because thou hast rejected the word of the Lord, he hath also rejected thee from being king" (1 Sam. 15:23). Saul pleaded with Samuel to reconsider and to come and worship (make sacrifices on behalf of Saul). Samuel refused because of the deep-seated root of rebellion that was in Saul. So when Samuel went to walk away, Saul grabbed ahold of his mantle (outer coat, or garment, which represents the anointing), ripping a piece of the prophet's mantle. Samuel turned and basically said, "That was prophetic, for your kingdom has been torn from you and you are no longer looked upon as king by God." (1 Sam. 15:26-27.)

Yet, Samuel yielded to Saul's persistence and went and worshipped. Saul begged him to do so in front of the elders of his people (15:30), in order to regain the favor of the people of Israel, with hopes to keep his kingdom. Saul was moved by the opinions of men and was a crowd pleaser.

The opposite was true of David. When Nathan confronted him with his sin, David confessed immediately, making no excuses. (2 Sam. 12:13.) When Saul was confronted with his sin, he said something like this, "Take not thy kingdom from me." But when David was confronted, he said, "Take not thy Holy Spirit from me" (Ps. 51:11). Saul did not want to be separated from the prestige of the kingdom, but David did not want to separated from the presence of God. Saul attempted to keep the sheep devoted to God. David offered himself to God as a sacrifice.

God said, "Ye are cursed with a curse." (Mal. 3:9a.) "Bring ye all the tithes into the storehouse, that there may be meat in mine house, and prove me [test me] now herewith, saith the Lord of hosts" (Mal. 3:10a). Why does He say, "Test me"? It's because the covenant is always activated by faith. The biggest thing that holds me back from being obedient is fear, which is the opposite of faith. You have to stop the fear and walk in faith.

"Prove me, test me." See, "If I will not open you the windows of heaven" (3:10b). Windows have primarily one purpose—to give you a vision. If you are a tither, you have a right to say, "Open the windows of heaven. Open the vision to reveal my destiny and to reveal my purpose. Show me who I'm to marry. Show me the city to live in. Show me what I'm to do." The only eternal reward in my life is that which I have done out of destiny and purpose.

The tither has open windows. They have a vision. A vision is the prophetic utterance of the words of God.[10] Ephesians 1:9 says when you have a vision, the mystery of the will of God is made known unto you, and that which you could not see, you can now see.

When you tithe, Malachi 3:11 says, the Lord "will rebuke the devourer for your sakes." The Lord Himself rebukes it. The devourer, literally means, "to eat a piece of" or "to slander."[11] The devourer can only be rebuked in your life by any other means other than the covenant, through the tithe. You can pray and fast all day and go to church 50 times in one week, but if it is a stronghold that is consuming your possessions, you can do nothing about. It is a demonic assignment and alignment against you that only the Lord can rebuke—through your tithe. The tithe releases you into covenant and redeems that which will break you–that devourer, the seed-eater and crippler.

So, the power is not broken because of your money! You can bring ten percent, but if you don't have faith in the covenant, you'll never walk in the benefits of the covenant. You have to have an understanding of what you are doing, why you are doing it, and how to activate it. Thank God for the covenant. Everything you need is in the covenant. There is healing for your body because of the covenant. Your children will come back home and your family will be restored because of the covenant. You're in your right mind because of the covenant. There's vision in the covenant. God's going to bless you and cause you to prosper because of the covenant. He's a good God, and the truth that YOU know liberates you and sets you free.

Keeping Things in Order, the Melchizedek Tithe

Our prosperity is dependent upon our relationship with God, through the covenant with Jesus. Prosperity is the wholeness, goodness, and fullness of God in our life. It comes through faith. It cannot be entered into with impure motives or selfish desires. If we give our tithe but do it with alternative motives—such as to be seen by others seeking public recognition (Matt. 6:1-4), or tell a lie about our giving (Acts 5:4)—we cannot receive the blessings. They are conditional upon obedience and covenant.

There is not a set pattern or method in which you must give to God. It is not a written code, a legal article, or a religious practice. It is to be a fresh, heartfelt approach of thanksgiving to God. There is not a pattern, but there is an order. In other words, there is an order by which Him will distribute His blessing. The order of worship is to approach God through covenant. Let me explain what I mean.

Everything you need life is in the covenant. The covenant is an order of redemption, love, and blessing. God redeemed us, and He blesses us because of His love. The sealing of the covenant is a sacrifice given to God. Abraham demonstrated his faith after defeating the kings in battle when he gave his tithes to Melchizedek, the king of Salem. (Gen. 14:18.) Salem is best identified with Jerusalem. (Psm. 76:2.) According to the Scriptures, this unknown king and priest is a type of Christ. (Psm. 110:4; Matt. 22:43.)

The author of Hebrews goes even further to compare him with Christ when emphasizing Melchizedek by interpretation with Messianic titles, such as the King of Righteousness and King of Peace (7:2). "Without father, without mother, without descent, having neither beginning of days, nor end of life; but made like unto the Son of God; abideth a priest continually" (7:3). This unique description typifies Christ by making an emphatic recognition of His God-like character and God-like origin.

He then proceeds to demonstrate 4 ways that the priestly order of Melchizedek is special and superior to the order of Aaron: (1) because Melchizedek is greater than Abraham, the father of Levi, for he blessed Abraham and received tithes from him instead of giving tithes to Abraham (Heb. 7:4-10); (2) because David predicted that the order of Melchizedek would replace the Levitical priesthood, showing that the latter was imperfect (7:11-19); (3) because of the divine oath behind it (7:20-22); and (4) and because of its permanence (7:23-25.)11

After the military expedition, Abraham returns with his booty and meets this priest-king of Salem, who apparently comes out to congratulate him on his victory, bringing bread and wine (the New Testament symbol of covenant); substance for the exhausted warriors and a symbol of gratitude for defeating his enemies; and as a result bringing peace, freedom, and prosperity.[12]

In the Genesis account Melchizedek is called "the priest of the most High God" (14:18, El Elyon in Hebrew).[13] This is hardly a title for a heathen foreigner or a pagan king-priest. He pronounces a poetic oracle over Abraham, a blessing acknowledging and invoking the only supreme, true God, who is the "possessor of heaven and earth" (14:19). I find this so amazing that a so-called Canaanite king who lived in a pagan religious world not only knew of the Most High God by name but also declared Him to be the only God!

The priestly blessing so impacted Abraham that he returned and gave a tenth of all that he had apprehended in battle. "Giving the tenth was a practical acknowledgment of the divine priesthood of Melchizedek; for the tenth was, according to the general custom, the offering presented to the Deity."[14]

Abraham further recognized the God of Melchizedek as the true God, for when the king of Sodom observed that the King of Salem gave a gift—bread and wine—he asked for his people only, and then offered all the riches from the booty of war. But Abraham refused and swore by an oath (lifting his hand) that he would not take anything, in order that no one could take credit for making him rich. Abraham did not want anything to do with the King of Sodom (a worldly, pagan king), but instead, he received the substance and the blessing from Melchizedek.

This is type and shadow of Christ reveals to us that Abraham made covenant (bread and wine) with Melchizedek, then received a priestly blessing, and reciprocated by giving a tenth of all he had. This is significant, because to understand the concept of covenant and tithe of the Melchizedek order, we must respond accordingly.

God intervened to allow 318 men to defeat four kings who had seized all the goods and carried all the people away, including Lot and his family. Abraham defended them and recovered all that was stolen. They not only saved Lot and his family, but they rescued all the people of the city of Sodom. This act of recompense and mercy was granted to the heathen. God is so good! He is always seeking to save the lost. (Luke 19:10.) We must go and do likewise; we must win the battle against Satan, not just for our loved ones but also for all those who are in cities. When you are convinced that God wants you, to recover all the enemy has stolen from you then He will give you your "Tampa."

Abraham gave his tenth to Melchizedek, whose priesthood was greater than the priesthood of Aaron. (Heb. 7:11.) This demonstration of worship was an act of covenant between Abraham and Melchizedek (a type and shadow of Christ). Jesus is our Melchizedek—our High Priest. So in a sense, Abraham gave his tithe to "Christ," our High Priest, out of devotion, not due to law. Tithing is not Old Testament, like some would try to emphasize, insinuating that it is no longer to be practiced. I will go even one step further: tithing was not instituted in the Mosaic Law or the Ten Commandments (Ex. 20:1-17). Tithing came before the law not after. In relation to the tithe, the Law was only to describe further the methods of distribution and explain its priestly role with the Levites—not to start an act of duty or a legal regulation. Tithing was not initiated through a commandment but through a covenant. Covenant denotes relationship.

Everything that remains comes through covenant. When you and I tithe, we are making covenant with Jesus. By giving to Him out of relationship and not regulations, we consummate covenant and receive His priestly blessing into our lives. When we tithe, give our first fruits, or the sacred, holy, devoted things to God, then He can sanctify "those things that are shaken, as of things that are made, that those things which cannot be shaken may remain" (Heb. 12:27b).

Final Thoughts

I want to finish with words of love and not condemnation. When it comes to teaching, the love approach will shine the light on things that have been hidden, but condemnation will turn out the lights and tell you to find your way out on your own. If you're not a tither or have tithed only "part-time," just repent. And repent doesn't just mean, "I'm sorry." Repentance means, "I change my mind." It means to make a 180-degree turn in your life. If you are a new Christian and you have never been privileged to hear about the tithe, you need to act upon truth. You're not responsible for what you don't know. Starting today, you will begin by giving a tenth to God. But remember, the emphasis is not just on the tenth; it is on the whole.

Now if you are a Christian, you have practiced tithing but have not been consistent, or at least you know that it is in God's Word but you have not been faithful, there is a way to redeem the tithe. In Leviticus, it says that if you have estimated your giving (27:27), the way to redeem (to make compensation or commutation) the tithe, that is to make it right, you are to show your act of repentance by adding a fifth (20 percent) to it. (Lev. 27:31.) Up until now you may have tried to justify or rationalize it, but now redeeming your tithe can liberate you. The Bible says, "Therefore to him that knoweth to do good, and doeth not, it becomes sin" (James 4:17).

You're not under any condemnation if you didn't have a full understanding of what tithe was in your life. Don't think, "Oh no, I've been inconsistent for the last 3 years, and now do I have to come up with 20 percent?" I believe we live under grace and mercy, so repent and go on with your life. But at the same time, I do believe when you have knowledge of something, then you can no longer walk in ignorance. You are responsible for what you know. "And ye shall know the truth, and the truth shall make you free" (John 8:32).

God came to give you abundant life. Living the abundant life means to be emotionally stable, spiritually strong, physically healed, financially whole, and perpetually prosperous, with your family fully intact. Now, you can begin to live the abundant life of Christ. Your prosperity does not depend upon you—just your obedience. The enemy would want nothing more than to keep you bound, broke, busted, and disgusted. But now, you have truth and new revelation on the principles of prosperity, the Abrahamic covenant, the Melchizedek tithe, and living the abundant life. "The thief comes only in order that he may steal and may kill and may destroy. I came that they may have and enjoy life, and have it in abundance—to the full, till it overflows" (John 10:10, Amp).

"Father, I thank you for your Word and for revealing your covenant. Seal the words penned in this book by the Holy Spirit and by the blood of the Lamb. Reveal each day the depth of your covenant to us so that we may walk in obedience to Your Word. I declare that it shall not escape the wombs of our spirits, but rather, it shall produce fruit for a bountiful harvest, in Jesus' name. Amen."

NOTES

Chapter One

1. *Strong's Exhaustive Concordance, Compact Edition,* (Grand Rapids, Michigan: Baker Book House), 1982, O. T. 1431.
2. *Vine's Expository Dictionary of Old and New Testament Words, Reference Library Edition,* (Iowa Falls: Iowa: Word Bible Publishers), 1981, "Wish".
3. *Word Meanings in the New Testament,* Ralph Earle, (Peabody, Massachusetts, Hendrickson Publishers, Inc.), 1974, page 454.
4. *Vine's Expository Dictionary of Old and New Testament Words, Reference Library Edition,* (Iowa Falls: Iowa: Word Bible Publishers), 1981, "Health".
5. *Theological Wordbook of the Old Testament,* Harris, Archer, Waltke, (Chicago, Illinois: Moody Press), vol. II, 1980, page 931
6. *Webster's 1828 Dictionary,* Electronic Version by Christian Technologies, Inc. (http://65.66.134.201/cgibin/webster/webster.exe?search_for_d:/inetpub/wwwroot/cgi-bin/webster/web1828=renewing).
7. *New International Dictionary of New Testament Theology,* Colin Brown, (Grand Rapids, Michigan: Zondervan) vol. III, 1986, page 674.
8. *Wycliffe Bible Dictionary,* (Peabody, Massachusetts: Hendrickson Publishers, Inc.),

1998, "Bosom."
9. *Christianity with Power,* Charles H. Kraft, (Ann Arbor, Michigan: Servant Publications), 1989, pages 109,110.
10. *Foundations of Pentecostal Theology,* Guy P. Duffield/N.M. Van Cleave, (Los Angeles, California: L.I.F.E. Bible College), 1987, page 210.

Chapter Three

1. Wycliffe Bible Dictionary, (Peabody, Massachusetts: Hendrickson Publishers, Inc.), 1998, "Shalom".
2. *Word Meanings in the New Testament,* Ralph Earle, (Peabody, Massachusetts, Hendrickson Publishers, Inc.), 1974, page 454.
3. *Vine's Expository Dictionary of Old and New Testament Words, Reference Library Edition,* (Iowa Falls: Iowa: Word Bible Publishers), 1981, "Worship."
4. *Vine's Expository Dictionary of Old and New Testament Words, Reference Library Edition,* (Iowa Falls: Iowa: Word Bible Publishers), 1981, "Defile, Defilement."

Chapter Four

1. *Strong's Exhaustive Concordance, Compact Edition,* (Grand Rapids, Michigan: Baker Book House), 1982, O. T. 4194.

Chapter Five

1. *Vine's Expository Dictionary of Old and New Testament Words, Reference Library Edition,* (Iowa Falls: Iowa: Word Bible Publishers), 1981, "Disciple."
2. *Vine's Expository Dictionary of Old and New Testament Words, Reference Library Edition,* (Iowa Falls: Iowa: Word Bible Publishers), 1981, "Continue."
3. *Strong's Exhaustive Concordance, Compact Edition,* (Grand Rapids, Michigan: Baker Book House), 1982, N. T. 4194.
4. *Vine's Expository Dictionary of Old and New Testament Words, Reference Library Edition,* (Iowa Falls: Iowa: Word Bible Publishers), 1981, pages 297, 298.
5. *Strong's Exhaustive Concordance, Compact Edition,* (Grand Rapids, Michigan: Baker Book House), 1982, O. T. 3045.
6. *Roget's Thesaurus,* " 2003, "Prosperity," http://thesaurus.reference.com/, June 23, 2003.
7. *Vine's Expository Dictionary of Old and New Testament Words, Reference Library Edition,* (Iowa Falls: Iowa: Word Bible Publishers), 1981, "Covenant."
8. *Zondervan Pictorial Encyclopedia of the Bible,* (Grand Rapids, Michigan: Zondervan Publishing), "Blessing", 1978, page 625.
9. *The JPS Torah Commentary, Genesis,* Nahum M. Sarna, (Philadelphia, New York, Jerusalem: The Jewish Publication Society), 1989, page 89.

Chapter Six

1. *Wycliffe Bible Dictionary,* (Peabody, Massachusetts: Hendrickson Publishers, Inc.), "Ur," 1998, page 1758,59.
2. *The New Manners and Customs of Bible Times,* Ralph Gower, (Chicago, Illinois: Moody Press), 1987, page 132.
3. *Wycliffe Bible Dictionary,* (Peabody, Massachusetts: Hendrickson Publishers, Inc.), "Haran," 1998, page 752,53.
4. *Manners and Customs in the Bible,* Victor H. Matthews, (Peabody, Massachusetts: Hendrickson Publishers), 1991, page 11.
5. *Manners and Customs in the Bible,* Victor H. Matthews, (Peabody, Massachusetts: Hendrickson Publishers), 1991, page 18.
6. *Strong's Exhaustive Concordance, Compact Edition,* (Grand Rapids, Michigan: Baker Book House), 1982, O. T. 4643.
7. *Wycliffe Bible Dictionary,* (Peabody, Massachusetts: Hendrickson Publishers, Inc.), "First fruits," 1998, page 611.
8. *Tyndale Old Testament Commentaries,* Joyce G. Baldwin, ((Downers Grove, Illinois: Inter-Varsity Press), 1972, page 245.
9. *Theological Wordbook of the Old Testament,* Harris, Archer, Waltke, (Chicago, Illinois: Moody Press), vol. I, 1980, page 75.
10. *Zonderan Pictorial Encyclopedia of the Bible,* (Grand Rapids, Michigan: Zondervan Publishing), vol. IV, 1978, page 889.

11. *Theological Wordbook of the Old Testament,* Harris, Archer, Waltke, (Chicago, Illinois: Moody Press), vol. I, 1980, page 39.
12. *Zonderan Pictorial Encyclopedia of the Bible,* (Grand Rapids, Michigan: Zondervan Publishing), vol. I, 1978, page 178.
13. *Keil & Delitzch, Commentary of the Old Testament,* (Peabody, Massachusetts: Hendrickson Publishers), vol. I, 1989, page 207.
14. *Keil & Delitzch, Commentary of the Old Testament,* (Peabody, Massachusetts: Hendrickson Publishers), vol. I, 1989, page 208.

ABOUT THE AUTHOR

Paula White. Known for her dynamic Bible teachings and preaching, her motivational delivery communicates the exciting message of Christ with sincerity and intensity. A much in demand speaker, she is also a profile author, evangelist, and founder of Paula White Ministries. She is also recognized for her ability to convey God's Word with practical reality concerning the important issues we all face today.

Paula White Today, her internationally televised program, is aired around the world on TBN, BET, Daystar and other major networks, ministering to those who are lost and hurting while instilling the transforming power of Jesus Christ.

She and her husband Randy White, pastor Without Walls International Church, a culturally diverse expression of some 18,000 members in Tampa, Florida where they reside. They have four children; Kristen, Angela, Brandon, and Bradley.